A SHORT INTRODUCTION TO THE OLD TESTAMENT PROPHETS

E. W. Heaton is a leading Old Testament scholar and the author of numerous books on the Old Testament, including *Everyday Life in Old Testament Times* and *The Hebrew Kingdoms*.

Other books by E. W. Heaton

Everyday Life in Old Testament Times
The Hebrew Kingdoms

Other books in this series

A Short History of the Bahá'í Faith by Peter Smith
A Short History of Buddhism by Edward Conze
A Short History of Islam by William Montgomery Watt
A Short History of Judaism by Lavinia and Dan Cohn-Sherbok
A Short Reader in Judaism by Lavinia and Dan Cohn-Sherbok

A Short Introduction to the
Old Testament Prophets

E. W. HEATON

ONEWORLD

OXFORD

A SHORT INTRODUCTION TO THE OLD TESTAMENT PROPHETS

Oneworld Publications
(Sales and Editorial)
185 Banbury Road
Oxford OX2 7AR
England

Oneworld Publications
(US Marketing Office)
PO Box 830, 21 Broadway
Rockport, MA 01966
USA

ISBN 1-85168-114-0

Printed and bound by
WSOY, Finland

For
Rachel
and our seventh grandchild
Sophie
who was born as this book was being revised

ACKNOWLEDGEMENT

The biblical quotations in this book (except as otherwise noted) are taken from the Revised Standard Version of the Bible, copyrighted 1946 and 1952 by the Division of Christian Education, United States National Council of Churches, and used by permission.

CONTENTS

PREFACE

I am greatly indebted to Novin Doostdar of Oneworld Publications for giving the 1977 edition of *The Old Testament Prophets* a new lease of life. The text has been revised throughout, and in the last two chapters I have added new material on the interpretation of prophecy – in scribal tradition, in apocalyptic circles, and in the early Church. The book, however, is still addressed to the student and general reader for whom it was originally intended, and so the footnotes, while giving full biblical references, have been kept free of the all-too-familiar display of secondary sources. I hope the new bibliography sufficiently indicates the works which underlie my exposition and that the student will find it useful as a guide to further reading.

Oxford, 1995   E. W. HEATON

ABBREVIATIONS

Chr.	Chronicles	Lam.	Lamentations
Col.	Colossians	Lev.	Leviticus
Cor.	Corinthians	Macc.	Maccabees
Dan.	Daniel	Mal.	Malachi
Deut.	Deuteronomy	Matt.	Matthew
Ecclus.	Ecclesiasticus	Mic.	Micah
Eph.	Ephesians	NEB	New English Bible
Esd.	Esdras	Neh.	Nehemiah
Exod.	Exodus	Num.	Numbers
Ezek.	Ezekiel	Obad.	Obadiah
Gal.	Galatians	Pet.	Peter
Gen.	Genesis	Prov.	Proverbs
Hab.	Habakkuk	Ps.	Psalms
Hag.	Haggai	REB	Revised English Bible
Heb.	Hebrews	Rev.	Revelation
Hos.	Hosea	Rom.	Romans
Isa.	Isaiah	Sam.	Samuel
Jer.	Jeremiah	Thess.	Thessalonians
Josh.	Joshua	Wisd.	Wisdom
Judg.	Judges	Zech.	Zechariah
Kgs.	Kings	Zeph.	Zephaniah

CHRONOLOGICAL TABLE

	UNITED KINGDOM		
1000 BC	David c.1000–961		
	Solomon c.961–922		
	SOUTHERN KINGDOM	NORTHERN KINGDOM	BOOKS (in approximate chronological order)
		Jeroboam I 922–901	
900 BC			
800 BC	Azariah (Uzziah) 783–742	Jeroboam II 786–746	Amos Hosea Isaiah Micah
		Fall of Northern Kingdom 721	
	Hezekiah 715–687		
700 BC	Josiah 640–609		Jeremiah Zephaniah
	Fall of Nineveh 612		Habakkuk Nahum
600 BC	Fall of Jerusalem 587 Exile 587–?		Ezekiel Obadiah Second Isaiah
	Cyrus conquers Babylon 539		I and II Kings
500 BC			Haggai Zechariah 1–8 Isaiah 56–66 Malachi
400 BC	Ezra? 397		Joel Jonah I and II Chronicles
	Alexander conquers Palestine 333		
300 BC			
200 BC	Antiochus Epiphanes 175–163 Desecration of the Temple 167		Ecclesiasticus Tobit Daniel

CHAPTER 1

Making Sense of the Old Testament

An English scholar has recently observed that 'Christianity is unique among the great religions in being born with a Bible in its cradle.' The infant Church quite evidently found the Old Testament a somewhat embarrassing birthday present and devoted a great deal of intellectual ingenuity to the problem of learning to live with it. The difficulties the early Christians faced are once again becoming acute, partly because the traditional ways by which the Church through the centuries has imposed an acceptable interpretation on the Old Testament are now discredited and, in English-speaking countries, because the Old Testament is no longer couched exclusively in the language of good King James. The Authorized Version of the Bible compounded beautiful prose with profound obscurity – and in so convincing and persuasive a way that cunning expositors had little difficulty in conjuring heavenly doctrines out of its earthy text. Modern translations have now brought inescapably to our attention just how very earthy the text of the Old Testament really is. The publication of the New English Bible, for example, provoked a correspondent to inform the editor of *The Times* that he could find nothing in it but 'an obscene chronicle of man's cruelty to man'.

The mellow religious patina deposited by devotional use and exposition through the centuries has now been decisively removed and we are (so to speak) confronted with the bare metal of the original. It turns out that it is not all pure gold; some of it is silver, some bronze, some iron and some alloy; some of it, indeed, is crude unrefined ore. And so the Old Testament does not shine, as it used to shine, and that means that when we look at it, we no longer see the reflection of our own faces. And that is disquieting. What we do see is more nearly what is really there – what the Old Testament really is – the complex product of a complex people, whose culture was not Western, like ours, but that of the ancient Near East between two and three thousand years ago. Modern translations do not, as is often supposed, bring the Old Testament closer to the modern world; they make it more distant and enable us to see that it belongs to an ancient culture quite different from our own. It is simply not the case that modern Christians now possess the Old Testament in their own current forms of speech; it is, rather, that the Old Testament is now making a bid to possess the modern Christian. The ancient scriptures have won their autonomy and now demand to be understood (as scholars have long acknowledged) in their own terms. How, then, may we make sense of them?

There would, of course, be no problem at all, were it not for the conviction that the Old Testament scriptures are not simply Jewish but also (in some sense) part of the self-revelation of the God and Father of Jesus Christ and therefore (in some sense) authoritative for Christians. There were those in the early days of the Church who were prepared to get rid of the problem by denying this conviction. This was the line taken by the notorious Marcion, a wealthy, second-century Mediterranean ship-owner. He has become the patron saint of many latter-day radical theologians, because he rejected the Old Testament *in toto* and declared that he could have no dealings with a God who was fickle, capricious, ignorant, despotic and cruel. It is highly significant that Marcion was unable to stop at the Old Testament and, with the courage born of his impeccable logic, he equally rejected all those parts of the New Testament he judged to be rooted in the Old – and that meant all the Gospels, except a bowdlerized version of St Luke, and all the other New Testament writings, except ten of St Paul's epistles. Marcion's hatchet work on the New Testament and the Church's subsequent hatchet work on Marcion together powerfully illustrate the fundamental conviction of the early Christians that (in some sense) they belonged to the Old Testament and it to them. It was one and the same God, who had created the world, given the Law to Moses and declared his purpose through the prophets, who had now, in these last days, spoken in his Son.[1] Throughout the succeeding centuries, right up to our own time, few things in the history of the Church are more impressive than its deep-seated but muddled belief that, despite all the problems, the Old Testament must be retained.

Up to the end of the Middle Ages, the Church kept the Old Testament in play principally (although not exclusively) by allegorical interpretation. This exegetical device is familiar to English readers from the chapter headings of the Authorized Version. It is found at its most imaginative in the Song of Solomon, where an anthology of secular love songs of no direct religious significance is made to speak of Christ and his Church.

Although for centuries allegorizing the Old Testament occupied some of the most acute and fertile minds in Christendom, although it enabled intelligent men to present the Jewish scriptures as a book for Christians, and although it is quite conceivable that they would have been jettisoned as 'a stale piece of antiquity' without it, nevertheless, as a method of *interpretation*, allegorical exegesis is simply a trick – a trick not untypical of the ingenuity of the Greeks who invented it – to make an authoritative text mean what you want it to mean, despite the fact that the actual words mean something quite different. It is impossible to avoid the judgement that throughout most of the Middle Ages the Old Testament was a puppet in the hands of the Christian ventriloquist and merely mouthed the received doctrines of the Church.

The complex intellectual and religious stirrings in Europe, for which the ambiguous labels 'Renaissance' and 'Reformation' may be allowed to serve, eventually effected the liberation of the Hebrew scriptures from their centuries-old bondage. Gingerly, now translated into the vernacular, the Old Testament began its chequered career in the modern world and its progress has been marked, step by step, by a stripping away of its medieval dress and an astonishingly illuminating exposure of what it undeniably is. However, it

1. Heb. 1. 1, 2; see pp. 170–1.

lost its traditional meaning before it lost its traditional authority. The result was, for good and ill, that the Law and the Prophets of Israel came directly to determine not only the piety but also the polity of Protestant Europe, and England became the 'People of the Book'. It was a book, however, over which every individual soon asserted the right to read in his or her own way. Now that the traditional interpretation had been abandoned with the allegorizing that had made it possible, each expositor came to claim for his or her own understanding no less than the authority of the Spirit. As the poet Dryden ironically observed:

> The Book thus put in every vulgar hand,
> Which each presumed he best could understand,
> The common rule was made the common prey
> And at the mercy of the rabble lay.
> The tender page with horny fists was galled,
> And he was gifted most that loudest bawled . . .
> This was the fruit the private spirit brought,
> Occasioned by great zeal and little thought.

Some Bible readers, however, *were* taking thought and it drove them to the conclusion (glimpsed many times before but never wholeheartedly accepted) that the Old Testament should be studied *like any other book*. Such was the seventeenth-century Dutch Jewish philosopher Spinoza, who is generally regarded as the Father of modern biblical scholarship. Biblical scholarship continues to be sustained by this simple principle: 'like any other book'. This now seems so obvious that it is almost impossible for us to appreciate how great a revolution it represented and how fundamental and prolonged a crisis it provoked on the question of biblical authority. Only a hundred years ago, for example, the future Dean of Chichester could still declare from the pulpit of the University Church in Oxford: 'The Bible is none other than the voice of Him that sitteth upon the throne. Every book of it, every chapter of it, every verse of it, every word of it, every syllable of it, every letter of it, is the direct utterance of the

Most High.' Although the preacher was denounced both in *The Times* and the House of Commons, the Jesse window at the west end of the University Church is still there to witness to his popularity.

The passions aroused by the new scholarship are best illustrated by the *cause célèbre* of Darwin and Genesis. It was in 1642 that John Lightfoot of Cambridge calculated from the biblical data that the creation of the first man had taken place in 4004 BC – to be more precise, on 23 October of that year at 9 o'clock in the morning. And that is how matters stood until the middle of the nineteenth century. Then came the geologists, who began to unearth fossils of somewhat greater antiquity, followed by the biologists who shocked Victorian society by connecting humankind with the ape. Darwin's *Origin of Species* was published in 1859 and his *Descent of Man* in 1871. It was in June 1860, at a meeting of the British Association in Oxford, that a clash took place between T. H. Huxley, who styled himself 'Darwin's bulldog', and Samuel Wilberforce, then Bishop of Oxford, which subsequently became the symbol of what was believed to be the inevitable conflict between science and religion. The exchange did credit to neither party. To bolster his conviction that 'the principle of natural selection is incompatible with the Word of God', the Bishop appealed to the delicate feelings entertained about ladies in Victorian England and challenged Huxley to state whether it mattered if his grandmother was descended from an ape no less than his grandfather. Huxley replied tartly that he would rather be descended from an ape than a bishop.

Now that the dust of this unseemly skirmish has settled, we can see that what Huxley was contending for was intellectual freedom and what Wilberforce was contending for was human dignity and that the first chapter of Genesis around which the controversy raged, understood as it is now understood, could have been properly appealed to in support of both convictions. Unhappily, it was understood differently in those days, as witness the Bishop of Ely, who affirmed in a standard commentary, published in 1871, that 'the history of Creation in Genesis . . . was very probably the ancient primeval record of the formation of the world . . . [which] may even have been communicated to the first man in his innocence'. No sooner had the bishop penned his innocent speculation about Adam, than he was confronted by a letter to the *Daily Telegraph* of 4 March 1875, which announced that Ashurbanipal's library at Nineveh had yielded a Babylonian *Epic of Creation* disturbingly similar to the account in Genesis.

Fortunately, none of these tirades succeeded in deflecting biblical scholars from their disturbing pursuits. They continued quietly to learn their languages, analyse their documents, establish their chronologies and excavate their sites. There can be no doubt that it is the systematic unearthing of the culture of the ancient Near East that has done most to confirm and forward the principle that the Bible must be read 'like any other book'. Modern translations of the scriptures are the most recent public monuments to the success of this fascinating intellectual enterprise. It is too early to say what the public is going to make of it. These new versions modernize the Old Testament only in the sense that they deprive contemporary readers of any devotional escape from the sheer foreignness of the original. If they move the readers at all, they move them to the ancient Near East, with no friendly guide to help them find their way about. What are they to make of so incredibly diverse a literature, spanning over a thousand years' history, compiled, moreover, by people who had no use for waste-paper baskets and so made changes in historical narratives, codes of law and collections of prophetic oracles, simply by adding their own version to what was already current?

The sheer muddle of the Old Testament is a delight to scholars, because it discloses the way in which Israelites thought and did their theology, but does it not seem a nonsense to the ordinary reader? It may be suspected that it always was a nonsense, but now, as presented by modern translations, it is an *obtruded* nonsense, without the sanctity of Latin, the cadences of King James, or the pious ingenuities of allegorizing to conceal the fact. When the Revised Version was published in 1881, Gladstone is reported to have said, 'You will sacrifice truth if you don't read it, and you will sacrifice the people if you do.' A century later, it is not irreverence but irrelevance which is likely to alienate the ordinary reader. Concerning precisely what, he or she is provoked to ask, does this ancient and largely unintelligible literature reveal the truth? Gone are the days when Luther could affirm that scripture is 'of itself most certain, easy to understand, and reliable, interpreting itself, [and so] proving, judging and explaining all other [writings] in everything'. Erasmus, his brilliant contemporary, held that the Bible was obscure; and Erasmus was right.

What then can be done about it? One is reluctantly forced to the conclusion that the Old Testament can fully be understood only by the kind of person who originally wrote it. And on this question there appears to be a widespread and serious misunderstanding. It is only too often assumed that the Old Testament was produced by simple folk with the mentality of tribesmen. The Old Testament, in fact, was produced by educated people and, for good or ill, it is by educated people that it must now be reinstated in the thinking of the Church. What, then, will they make of it?

Theologians have been slow to learn from biblical scholarship that the scriptures do not contain a static deposit of normative doctrines; what they do contain is written evidence of a living community constantly responding to changing historical circumstances under the guidance of its transmitted religious traditions. These traditions, embodied in many different kinds of literature, were always reinterpreted by Israel's own teachers to help bring about a response from the community at points of significant historical change. But – and this is a fact of major importance – the method of reinterpretation they adopted was not to obliterate the received traditions, not to scrap the old writings, but rather *to make additions to them*. That is why the material of the Old Testament comes to us (as it were) in duplicate and triplicate, in highly complex bits and pieces. To recognize this basic fact, to discover that the Old Testament is an accumulation of successive and now juxtaposed versions of tradition, is to grasp the fundamentally *historical* character of Israel's theological understanding.

The theologians of Israel were not concerned to articulate *ideas* about God that would be valid at all times and in all places – ideas of the kind we might now distil from their writings for our own individual use. On the contrary, the theologians of Israel were in the most literal sense the theologians of *Israel*; that is to say, they were concerned to understand and express the relationship between God and their people, as they stood in particular and successive historical situations. For them (although they would not have used such an abstraction) history was reality; history was the medium both of God's activity and of Israel's response; history was the mode of God's life. They believed that the historical community of Israel had been created and preserved to be the focus of that life – the point at which God's ultimate purpose in and for history was openly and specifically manifest.

Among Israel's theologians, the prophets were distinctive in recognizing the 'scandal' of this particularity. They were acutely aware of the tension between their belief in the sovereignty of God in *all* history and their belief in the sovereignty of God as particularly focused in the history of their own community. That is why they looked for the resolution of this tension in the future. They called it the coming of the Kingdom, when *all* history would become unambiguously what from the beginning it was intended to be – the history of God, the non-resistant medium of God's activity and the manifest mode of his life.

If some such analysis of what is happening in the Old Testament be accepted, then the familiar label 'The Old Testament' seriously obscures its significance. It represents the scriptures of Israel as comprising a canon of religious literature that is unified and doctrinally authoritative; it represents it, that is to say, as a closed book. On the other hand, Israel's scriptures, understood as the unique historical witness to the unique historical dealings of God with his people, so far from being a closed book, are not a book at all; they are, rather, the record of an unfinished pilgrimage.

It cannot, of course, be claimed that all parts of the Hebrew scriptures are equally valuable in illuminating this pilgrimage. However, once we have grasped the essential key – God's dealing with his people in and through the totality of their historical existence – the whole incredibly diverse record may be studied with profit and without recourse to the artificial device of allegorizing and other comparably bogus methods of interpretation. Much of this ancient literature will be found to illuminate the activity of God in a merely negative way, that is, by the evidence it affords of Israel's attempts to withdraw from its pilgrimage, by, for example, its elaboration of religious institutions, in imitation of its neighbours in the ancient Near East. But all this dragging and distortion, all this unwillingness on the part of Israel to accept the risk of pilgrimage, is inseparable from the economy of God, who (as Christians also believe) discloses his purpose, not through the unmediated communication of infallible truths, nor through the blinding light of miraculous signs, but through the messiness of life as it is.

Nevertheless, seen in the context of the religious culture of the ancient Near East, as it is now seen more clearly than ever before, the pilgrimage of Israel, guided by the Law and the Prophets, emerges as a historical phenomenon without precedent or parallel. Here was a people daring to make the gamble of faith in a decisive breakaway from all the securities of religion as it was then understood, with its divinely validated sanctuaries and its divinely ordained priesthoods, its mythological assurances and its infallibly effective rites and ceremonies.

It was the prophets, in particular, who taught Israel to trust God as he was encountered in everyday human existence, where by definition there can be no certainty and no resting place. Despite the familiar claim of the textbooks, no such thing as 'prophetic religion' ever existed, since any kind of religion must offer a minimum of stable practice and reliable programme. For the radical prophets of Israel, nothing in the last analysis (and it was their distinctive contribution always to follow through their insight to the last analysis) was stable and reliable, except the sovereign purpose of God himself. This was disclosed in faith through his historical dealings with Israel, but it never found fulfilment in Israel's historical existence.

The community of Israel, thus oriented towards the future, was the historical matrix of the ministry of Jesus and of that astonishing re-formation which was its immediate consequence. When the first Christians annexed prophecies and other parts of the Hebrew scriptures and brought them into relation with Jesus of Nazareth, declaring 'This is that which was spoken by the prophet',[2] they were not merely and arbitrarily imposing new meaning on the old prophetic words for ephemeral apologetic purposes. They were doing something much more profound. In the first place, they were expressing their conviction that the new Christian community was continuous with the community of Israel, because the coming of Christ was an event in the history of God with his people (as the speeches in Acts and St Paul in Romans 9–11 so clearly affirm). In the second place, they were claiming that it was an event of so extraordinary a character that it actualized not only a new situation in the history of God with Israel, but also actualized in advance, as it were, that future and final situation in the history of God with the world to which the prophets of the Old Testament had looked forward. Of course, the first Christians were not the only Jews of the time to claim that their own community was the new Israel of the Final Age. As the Dead Sea Scrolls have clearly established, the sectarians of Qumran also updated the Old Testament scriptures with their own version of 'This is that which was spoken by the prophet.'[3]

In the last resort, the question about the Church's retention of the Old Testament is basically a question about the import-

2. Acts 2. 16: see pp. 162–71.
3. See pp. 159–60.

ance Christianity attaches to history. To keep it is to be committed to the view that Christian theology is and must remain the theology of a historical community and, in the last analysis, a theology of history. Such a view of the distinctive nature of Christian theology not only permits the full use of that historical–critical scholarship, which it would now be intellectual suicide to evade or deny; it emphatically demands it. The result must be that the distance between the Old Testament world and our own will become ever more obvious. This is not a matter for regret if we take history with theological seriousness, if, indeed, we accept it as the mode of God's being and life.

Before we affirm '*This* is that which was spoken by the prophet', before, that is to say, we affirm the continuity between the Christian community and the community of Israel, we must ask '*What* is that which was spoken by the prophets?' and try to grasp by critical investigation Israel's successive responses and successive traditions in the succession of history. By this means, without any evasion or doctoring of the facts, it is possible to make sense of the Old Testament, to learn a good deal of what is involved in being the People of God and to discern a sense of direction which provides as much of a norm as people on pilgrimage should need or desire.

CHAPTER 2

The Books of the Prophets

We may start our survey of the prophetic writings with a modern translation of the Old Testament in front of us, its pages open at the place where Isaiah begins. At our right hand we find three large books (Isaiah, Jeremiah and Ezekiel), two small books (Lamentations and Daniel), and twelve tracts of unequal length, each with a name at its head.

Daniel and Lamentations may be isolated immediately, since in the Hebrew Bible both these works are placed, not with the prophets, but in that miscellaneous group of Old Testament books called 'The Writings'.[1] This is obviously where Lamentations properly belongs, since it is made up of five dirge-like psalms, describing with a wealth of graphic detail the fall of Jerusalem in 587 BC. The ascription of the work to Jeremiah in the title lacks good authority, although it was probably composed by one of his contemporaries.

The book of Daniel is also out of place among the prophets. Its popular stories and highly symbolic visions were written in loyal scribal circles (related in many ways to the sect brought to light by the discovery of the Dead Sea Scrolls), when the very existence of the Jewish community was threatened by the persecuting Greek king, Antiochus IV Epiphanes, during the years 167–164 BC. It is a document of immense spiritual courage and great theological interest, but only confusion has resulted from its being read as the prophetic book *par excellence*. The ancient Egyptian device adopted by its author of addressing his contemporaries through the medium of an ancient sage has

---

1. The Writings include: Psalms, Proverbs, Job, Song of Solomon, Ruth, Lamentations, Ecclesiastes, Esther, Daniel, Ezra, Nehemiah and Chronicles.

encouraged the erroneous notion that prediction rather than proclamation was the primary business of the prophet. Its importance for our study lies in its distinctive reinterpretation of the prophets' teaching about the coming of the Kingdom of God.[2]

In this rapid survey, we shall therefore be concerned only with the three large books (Isaiah, Jeremiah and Ezekiel) and the twelve small tracts. The name given to the latter collection – the 'Minor Prophets' – is appropriate only to their size, for with the three books of the other group – the 'Major Prophets' – they represent the literary record of one of the most remarkable phenomena known to the historians of religion.

THE MINOR PROPHETS

We may start our exploration with HOSEA, one of the twelve minor prophets, and then work forward. The prophet, who is the only Northern Israelite whose sayings have been preserved, taught in the second half of the eighth century (from about 750–730 BC), when the prosperous kingdom of Israel was heading towards its destruction at the hands of Assyria in 721 BC. It is obvious that the fourteen chapters before us have been collected by somebody other than Hosea, since the first of them is biographical. The combination of biographical and autobiographical material in one and the same book, together with a number of intrusive references to Judah, is a fairly clear indication that the work has passed through the hands of an editor.[3] It is also worth noticing that the translators have been forced to include many variant readings in the notes at the foot of each page – a sure indication that the Hebrew text has come down to us in a rather bad state of preservation.

We know nothing of JOEL, whose name heads the next

2. See pp. 157–62.
3. The chief editorial additions in Hosea are: 1. 7; 1. 10–2. 1; 2. 16–20, 21–3; 3. 5; 4. 15; 5. 5; 6. 11; 8. 14; 10. 11; 11. 12; 12. 2; 14. 1–9.

book, except that he was the son of Pethuel (and that is not very helpful). The evidence supplied by the work itself, however, makes it plausible to ascribe it to a prophet *writing* about 400 BC. This dating is confirmed by the author's extensive borrowings from his predecessors[4] – a feature which characterizes the literary and more derivative prophecy of the period following the Exile of the Jews in Babylon in the sixth century BC.

We come now to the very important book of AMOS. Again, we know nothing of his parents, his family or his friends, and nothing of his connections with the prophets who came before him. The sparse biographical notes in the book (1. 1; 7. 14) suggest thate was a sheep-farmer from the east of Judah, who owned some land in the hill-country, where he cultivated sycamore figs. His social status is peculiarly difficult to determine, but so articulate a critic of the corruption of urban society can hardly have been an uneducated peasant.

Scholars argue about the exact date of Amos' ministry. It certainly came within the reign of Jeroboam II (786–746 BC), but within this period some favour aearly date (about 760 BC) and some a later one, when it was beginning to be obvious that Assyria would soon be in the field again threatening Israel's independence. We shall not be far wrong if we think of Amos as leaving his sheep and sycamores about 750 BC to denounce in the northern kingdom of Israel what Sir John Falstaff (as he reviewed his ragged recruits) called 'the cankers of a calm world and a long peace'. For about half a century, Israel had been unmolested by the great powers, and the resulting period of prosperity had given the unscrupulous speculators and get-rich-quicks their golden opportunity. Israel's decay, so far from being held in check by religious principles, was, in

4. In the following passages it is Joel who appears to be the borrower: 1. 15 (Isa. 13. 6); 2. 2 (Zeph. 1. 15); 2. 3 (Isa. 51. 3; Ezek. 36. 35); 2. 10 (Isa. 13. 10); 2. 32 (Obad. 17); 3. 10 (Isa. 2. 4; Mic. 4. 3); 3. 16 (Amos 1. 2; Isa. 13. 13); 3. 17 (Isa. 52. 1).

fact, being hastened by the superstitious and futile cult which flourished at the local sanctuaries. The state of the country was ruinous, but it needed a prophet of the courage and calibre of Amos to bring home to the people that they were not only in danger but doomed to destruction. God had rejected them and was about to give effect to his judgement.

It is very remarkable that we have any record at all of the sermons of a man who preached so radical and so unpopular a message over 2,500 years ago. How the discourses of Amos actually came to be preserved is a matter about which scholars can only speculate. We do not know whether Amos had either disciples or secretary, but the preservation of his message proves beyond dispute that he was not an isolated voice crying in the wilderness. How much (if anything) the prophet himself set down in writing, or revised, so to speak, before publication, we have no means of discovering. Here and there, a touch of irony strongly suggests that we are in close touch with the original author and it is clear that one master spirit has left its stamp on the bulk of the book. It is equally clear, however, that we owe some small parts of it to the schoolmen of succeeding centuries, who preserved the teaching of all the great prophets.[5]

Despite the long process of reinterpretation and literary development through which the book has passed, it still bears the marks of its origin in the spoken word. The short paragraphs (or 'oracles') of which it is composed are clearly related to the prophet's style of preaching, although the order of these oracles as they are now arranged is almost certainly the work, not of Amos, but of his editors. They have sometimes been grouped according to their subject matter, but, more often, they have been strung together without much thought of logical or chronological order. This editorial method (or lack of it) explains why the prophetic books are so disconnected and difficult to read and why many of them

5. Amos 1. 1, 2; 1. 9–12; 2. 4, 5; 3. 7; 4. 13; 5. 8, 9; 8. 8; 9. 5, 6; 9. 8–15; see pp. 148–52.

contain passages from an altogether different source. A care-free attitude to authorship and literary integrity was, of course, universal in the ancient world and it finds further illustration in the next of the minor prophets – the exilic fragment of OBADIAH, which is the shortest and perhaps the least illuminating book in the Old Testament. It consists basically of a not very edifying denunciation of Edom (vv. 1–18), which exploited Israel's weakness after the fall of Jerusalem in 587 BC; to this, a post-exilic editor has appended a promise of Israel's restoration (vv. 19–21).

The book of JONAH, which follows, is usually dated about 350 BC. It is unique among the prophetic books in being a work of didactic fiction – a kind of extended parable – written round the name of one of the ancient prophets (mentioned in II Kings 14. 25). The great fish (it is not called a whale) was just the sort of fantastic wonder in which the ancient story-tellers delighted and here it is commandeered as a bizarre form of transport for the petulant prophet. The dramatic conversion of the shipwrecked sailors and the whole popula-tion of Nineveh to the worship of the one true God exposes to ridicule the nationalistic religious tradition which Jonah represents and affirms that the God of Israel is – as the splendid formula puts it – 'a gracious and compassionate God, long-suffering, ever constant, always ready to relent and not inflict punishment'.[6] The final editor of the book, considering that a psalm would further enhance the tale, interpolated what is now the second chapter.

MICAH, a peasant farmer of Moresheth-gath in Judah, whose name heads the next collection of oracles, was respon-sible for the material now contained in the first three chapters of the book. As a contemporary of Isaiah, Micah exposed the depravity of both the northern and southern kingdoms dur-ing the last quarter of the eighth century BC. The remainder of the book is a mixed compendium of oracles, which for the most part express the hope of people living in exile that they would be restored to their own land, there to enjoy the

6. Jonah 4. 2 (REB).

blessings of the Reign of God.[7] Once again, we are reminded how it is only our failure to appreciate Hebrew literary methods which has given currency to the absurd notion that it is more pious to ascribe all the contents of a book to the 'title-prophet' than to welcome the aid of scholarly analysis. The complaint we may justly make against some of the earlier critical scholars is not that they 'carved up' the books of the Bible, but that they were wedded to the strange idea that a piece of biblical literature is intrinsically more valuable if we can name its author. The result was that they often over-looked the profound importance of anonymous prophecy. Their presuppositions are well illustrated, for example, by the many attempts to prove that 6. 1–8 is a genuine fragment of Micah's preaching. The passage, of course, stands in its own right, whatever its origin, as an illuminating summary of prophetic faith, requiring no further authentication.

The book NAHUM, which follows as we turn the pages, has very little spiritual significance. It combines fragments of an acrostic poem (1. 2–8) with a magnificent but terrible ode, celebrating the imminent collapse of Nineveh, the capital of Assyria, in 612 BC. A modern translation will help us recapture something of the prophet's grim realism, as he gloats over the dismembering of Israel's tyrannical oppressor. Despite the conventional prophetic formula in 2. 13 and 3. 5, it must be admitted that this book is far removed from the prophetic tradition of Amos and his successors and those who seek its origin and purpose in a liturgical context may well be working on the right lines.[8]

A cultic origin has been suggested also for the book of HABAKKUK, of which the first two chapters deal with the rise

7. This interpretation of Micah as a prophet of unmitigated judgement assumes the following critical conclusions about the authenticity of the oracles ascribed to him: (a) chapters 1–3 (with the exception of 2. 12, 13) derive from Micah himself; (b) chapters 4–5 and 7. 8–20, which promise the restoration of Jerusalem, the in-gathering of the exiles, the destruction of Israel's enemies, and the reign of a Davidic king in an age of peace, had their origin after 587 BC; (c) 6. 1–7.6 is unlikely to be the work of Micah.

8. See pp. 34–5.

of the Chaldeans, who were the founders of the Neo-Babylonian empire, and the problem raised by the suffering of the righteous at the hands of the wicked. It may be dated tentatively about 600 BC, except for the psalm of the third chapter, which is usually ascribed to an author of the post-exilic age. The earliest known commentary on this book, probably written in the second half of the first century BC, was one of the Dead Sea Scrolls discovered in 1947.[9] It may be no mere accident that it deals only with the first two chapters and shows no knowledge of the concluding psalm.

The core of the next book, ZEPHANIAH, appears to have originated towards the end of the seventh century BC before the religious reforms of King Josiah. The fearless radicalism of Amos is echoed in the prophet's denunciation of the corrupt leaders of Jerusalem for their idolatrous religious practices and their callous oppression of the poor. He announces that a great day of reckoning – the Day of the Lord – is imminent. The editorial elaborations that have shaped the book as we now have it are difficult to identify with confidence, but they testify to the continuing relevance of the prophet's championship of the poor and unshaken confidence in the righteousness of God.[10]

The book of HAGGAI, which follows, derives originally from a prophet attached to the priestly establishment of Jerusalem and is different from anything we have encountered so far. Its five reported declarations dated in 520 BC[11] are addressed not to the community at large, but to individuals (the governor Zerubbabel and the high-priest Joshua) and their main purpose is to promote the rebuilding of the Temple and by this means inaugurate a new age of salvation.

This restoration is one of the main interests of the next prophet, ZECHARIAH, whose own work is to be found in seven bizarre visions, dated between 520 and 518 BC, affirming his conviction that God will reinstate the worship of the Temple

9. See pp. 159–60.
10. Editorial elaboration may be detected in 1. 2, 3; 2. 8–11; 3. 14–20.
11. (*a*) Hag. 1. 1–14; (*b*) 2. 15–19; (*c*) 2. 1–9; (*d*) 2. 10–14; (*e*) 2. 20–3.

and establish Zerubbabel and Joshua, as king and and high-priest respectively.[12] Zechariah and Haggai are linked together in the memoir of Ezra and their oracles have been consolidated in a single framework by a later editor, who belonged, perhaps, to the circle of teachers who produced the books of Chronicles.[13] It is generally agreed that the last six chapters of the book (9–14) are not the work of Zechariah, although scholarly opinion has not crystallized to a more precise dating for them than the fourth or third century BC. Although anonymous and difficult to interpret, these later oracles of catastrophe and hope bear witness to a confidence in God's ultimate victory in the world with a vigour seldom surpassed in the Old Testament.

The last of the twelve minor prophets confirms the view that the names at the head of the various books are sometimes little more than an editorial convenience and by no means always describe the author of the succeeding oracles. MALACHI is simply the Hebrew for 'my messenger'.[14] These anonymous oracles were delivered about 460 BC. It will be noticed that the prophet has largely abandoned the former method of direct proclamation and now discusses current issues in a question-and-answer presentation of his message. We get the impression that he was a faithful and modest teacher, faced with despondency in his community and with the degeneration despondency breeds – slovenly worship, corrupt legal practice, divorce, social injustice and cynicism.[15]

THE MAJOR PROPHETS

We come now to the second phase of our rapid exploration of the prophetic writings and glance at the major prophets – the books of Isaiah, Jeremiah and Ezekiel. When no two scholars

12. (*a*) Zech. 1. 7–17; (*b*) 1. 18–21; (*c*) 2. 1–5; (*d*) 3. 1–4. 14; (*e*) 5. 1–4; (*f*) 5. 5–11; (*g*) 6. 1–8.
13. Ezra 5. 1; 6. 14; Hag. 1. 12–15; Zech. 1. 1–6; 7. 1–8. 23; see pp. 140–1.
14. Mal. 3. 1; cf. Hag. 1. 13.
15. Mal. 2. 4–7; 3. 1–4. His indebtedness to Deuteronomy has led to the suggestion that the author may have been a Levite.

are agreed about many of the hundred-and-one literary problems that they inevitably raise, it will be obvious that we cannot hope to do more than eliminate some of the difficulties which stand in the way of ordinary intelligent reading.

The book of ISAIAH is a vast and very untidy anthology containing: (*a*) oracles from Isaiah, the son of Amoz, whose prophetic activity in Jerusalem continued intermittently from about 742 BC to the end of the century; (*b*) oracles from an anonymous prophet (usually called Second- or Deutero-Isaiah), who was a member of the Jewish community living in Babylon about 540 BC; and (*c*) a large number of important miscellaneous passages of which the oracles contained in chapters 56–66 form a fairly unified group, reflecting the unsettled conditions in Jerusalem in the years following the return from exile.

The material which represents the preaching of Isaiah of Jerusalem is roughly that which remains in chapters 1–39, when we have identified as insertions made by later editors and interpreters such passages as the extract from II Kings 18. 13–20. 19 in chapters 36–9, the poems of final judgement and deliverance in chapters 24–7 and 34–5, most of the oracles of doom against foreign nations in chapters 13–23, and various sections which clearly reflect the outlook of the period following the fall of Jerusalem in 587 BC. It would be wholly mistaken to suppose that these passages from writers later than Isaiah can be dismissed as unimportant glosses. They are no less significant than (say) the eighteenth-century additions we may detect in an Elizabethan house. They have their meaning both as part of the final composition and as witnesses to the outlook of their own period. It is important, nevertheless, that we should attempt to isolate the oracles which may be attributed to the prophet Isaiah himself.[16]

16. The identification of the primary nucleus deriving from Isaiah himself is a delicate critical task from which no more than general agreement may be expected. The following selection of oracles commands considerable support among scholars: 1. 2–9; 1. 10–17; 1. 18–20; 1. 21–6; 2. 6–22; 3. 1–7, 13–15; 3. 16, 17, 24–4. 1; 5. 1–7; 5. 8–24; 6. 1–13; 7. 1–9; 7. 10–17; 7. 18–22; 8. 1–4; 8. 5–8;

Many of them are connected with *three* major crises which erupted in Judah during the last forty years of the eighth century BC. The *first* crisis occurred in 734 BC, when King Ahaz sought the protection of Assyria against a coalition of Damascus and Israel.[17] The *second* crisis was provoked by King Hezekiah's repeated attempts to assert his independence from Assyria, latterly in reliance on Egypt.[18] The *third* and final crisis was Assyria's crushing reply to Judah's rebellion in 701 BC, when Jerusalem was besieged and very nearly captured.[19]

If we are daunted by these literary complexities, we may take heart from the knowledge that the text of this untidy book has been transmitted with amazing fidelity through the centuries. Only a few years ago, the most ancient witness to the Hebrew text of Isaiah was no earlier than the tenth century AD. In 1947, however, the sensational discovery among the Dead Sea Scrolls of a beautifully preserved scroll containing the whole of the book (chs. 1–66) pushed back our evidence of its text over a thousand years – perhaps to the second century BC. It is astonishing and reassuring to learn that the traditional medieval manuscripts, upon which our translations hitherto had to rely, have preserved a text agreeing to a remarkable extent with that of the Dead Sea scroll. Thus we have been brought nearer than the greatest optimist ever dared hope to the time when the prophet's editors first completed their book.

The superb series of poems which make up chapters 40–55 of the book of Isaiah (so-called Second Isaiah) are the work of an anonymous prophet who lived among his compatriots exiled in Babylon a century and a half after the death of Isaiah

16. (*contd.*) 8. 11–15; 8. 16–18; 9. 8–21 (with 5. 25–30); 10. 1–3; 10. 5–15; 10. 27–32; 14. 24–7; 14. 28–31; 17. 1–6; 18. 1–6; 20. 1–6; 22. 1–14; 22. 15–19; 28. 1–4, 7–13; 28. 14–22; 28. 23–9; 29. 1–4, 6; 29. 9–12; 29. 13, 14; 29. 15, 16; 30. 1–5; 30. 8–17; 31. 1–3; 31. 4; 32. 9–14.

17. Most of the oracles in chapters 1–3 and 5–8, with 9. 8–21 and 17. 1–6.

18. Isa. 14. 28–31; 18. 1–6; 20. 1–6; 28. 1–13, 14–22; 29. 1–14; 30. 1–5, 8–17; 31. 1–4.

19. Isa 1. 4–9; 10. 5–15; 14. 24–7; 22. 1–14; 32. 9–14.

of Jerusalem. Cyrus, the King of Persia, who conquered Babylon in 539 BC and allowed the Jewish exiles to return home, is twice mentioned explicitly in the book (44. 28; 45. 1). The prophet addressed his compatriots just before they were liberated by their new ruler.[20] We know nothing about him,[21] except that he was a man of literary genius and unprecedented theological insight, who matched the hour of the Jews' greatest need, when they were in danger of forsaking the faith of their ancestors. He met the dejection of the exiled Judaeans with undaunted confidence in God's sovereignty and urged that the despair of the present time was only the prelude to their restoration to Jerusalem and to the New Age that God was about to inaugurate. As these sixteen chapters are singularly free from the surface difficulties and many of the knotty historical problems that other prophetic books present, we can – with pleasure and immense profit – read the whole work at a single sitting. To appreciate the tremendous range of the prophet's vision is the first step towards understanding his message; and the lyrical and dramatic style of which he was so great a master grips the reader with a peculiar intensity.

The last eleven chapters of Isaiah (56–66), usually referred to as 'Third Isaiah', reflect the frustrations and conflicts of the Jerusalem community at the end of the sixth century BC, after some of the exiles had started to trickle home from Babylon. It is probable that this collection of oracles became attached to Isaiah 40–55 because it originated in the teaching of a group of disciples of Second Isaiah who wished to apply his confident message to their own circumstances.[22] Although they were loyal to the Temple and its establishment,[23] they encountered violent opposition from powerful sections of the community.[24]

20. Isa. 41. 2–4; 41. 25; 45. 1–6; 45. 13; 46. 11; 48. 14, 15.
21. Unless he is depicted in the 'Servant Songs'; see pp. 123–4.
22. See especially: Isa. 57. 14–21; 60. 1–22; 61. 1–3, 4–11; 62. 1–12; 65. 17–25.
23. Isa. 56. 7; 60. 7, 13; 62. 9; 63. 18–19.
24. Isa. 56. 9–57. 13; 65. 1–7, 8–15; 66. 1–5.

JEREMIAH, to whose book we now turn, had a secretary – Baruch – and he made all the difference.[25] The work moves in a superficially orderly fashion from oracles (chs. 1–25) to stories of the prophet's ministry (chs. 26–45), followed by a compendium of passages (not by Jeremiah) on foreign nations (chs. 46–51). The book ends with a historical appendix (ch. 52) taken by an editor from II Kings (24. 18–25. 21, 27–30). The main body of the work (chs. 1–45) has been fairly thoroughly edited. This means that, while relatively few passages have to be wholly discounted when we try to reconstruct Jeremiah's own preaching,[26] we find that a great part of the material has been 'touched up' and reinterpreted – probably by the schoolmen who produced the book of Deuteronomy. We can therefore always be fairly sure of the prophet's general meaning, but there is often room for more than one opinion when we come to finer details. It is the poetic oracles (rather than the prose narratives) that give us the most reliable insight into the complexities of the prophet's mind. Jeremiah witnessed the final collapse of Judah as an independent kingdom and went into exile in Egypt a broken man and an apparent failure. It is, however, to his forty years' ministry (626–587 BC) that we turn for the clearest evidence of the permanent significance of pre-exilic prophecy.

EZEKIEL, the last of the books of the major prophets, is the despair of both Old Testament scholars and the ordinary reader. We have to choose between making a frank admission that these forty-eight chapters represent a compilation of which the proper analysis has so far escaped us, and accepting as sole author a prophet to whom we must attribute an extraordinary diversity of experience. The physical and spiritual gymnastics with which the second choice credits Ezekiel obviate our literary problems only by raising much more difficult questions of their own. As the book now stands, it

25. See pp. 26–7.
26. The following passages are the principal additions to Jeremiah's own oracles: 2. 19–22, 29, 30, 33–7; 3. 14–18; 5. 18, 19; 6. 16–19; 7. 24–8.3; 10. 1–16; 11. 1–17; 12. 7–17; 16. 10–21; 17. 5–13, 19–27; 23. 3–8, 33–40; 30. 8–11, 16–24; 31. 7–14, 23–30, 38–40; 32. 16–44; 33. 1–26. See pp. 112–13, 142.

includes: (*a*) oracles apparently delivered in Jerusalem before the fall of the city in 587 BC (chs. 1–24); (*b*) oracles against foreign nations (chs. 25–32); (*c*) oracles apparently delivered in Babylon describing the coming restoration of the exiles to Jerusalem (chs. 33–9); and (*d*) an idealized vision of the restored Jerusalem, with a detailed 'blue-print' of the new Temple, its plan, priesthood and worship (chs. 40–8).

It is clear that the book has been finally structured according to a pattern we also find in the books of Isaiah and Jeremiah,[27] but it is far from clear in what circles the prophet's teaching was originally transmitted, edited and amplified. The theme recurrent in these chapters of 'the glory of the God of Israel', moving from one place to another,[28] suggests a connection with the writers responsible for the priestly version of the story of Moses.[29]

On the face of it, Ezekiel's call to the prophetic ministry came to him in Babylon in 593 BC among the exiles of the first deportation of 597 BC and he never returned to Palestine. The fact that many of his prophecies are addressed to the people of Jerusalem has led some scholars to the view that the work of a prophet, who was a contemporary of Jeremiah, has been arbitrarily transferred by an editor from Jerusalem to Babylon, and other scholars to the compromise of postulating for the prophet a double ministry – first in Jerusalem and afterwards in Babylon. Nobody with any respect for the difficulties of historical reconstruction will wish to dogmatize in the present chaotic state of scholarly discussion. Although the personality and the characteristic teaching of the prophet must remain uncertain, it may fairly be assumed that the bulk of the material now ascribed to him gives us a reliable insight into the kind of teaching that helped the exiles to survive in Babylon and to shape the future of Judaism in the post-exilic period.

We are now in a position to review this succession of prophets, bearing in mind that no one figure may be said to

27. See p. 155.
28. Ezek. 1. 28; 9. 3; 10. 3–5, 18–19; 11. 22, 23; 45. 1–5.
29. Exod. 16. 7, 10; 24. 15–18; 40. 34–5; Num. 14. 10; 16. 19, 42.

have embodied – or even to have influenced – the *whole* religious life of his age. In the *pre-exilic period*, we have in the eighth century: Amos, Hosea, Micah and Isaiah; and in the seventh century: Zephaniah, Nahum, Habakkuk and Jeremiah. The imperial background of the former group is dominated by Assyria and of the latter by Babylon.

Thoughts of restoration and reconstruction were uppermost in the prophecy of the *exilic period*: Second Isaiah, Ezekiel, Isaiah 56–66, Haggai and Zechariah. *After 500 BC*, Malachi, Joel and Jonah show the prophetic flame still alight but flickering. There is, in addition, a vast quantity of anonymous oracles from different periods after the fall of Jerusalem, now interpolated in the various books.

Such a survey as this should call into question and cause us to modify any view of prophecy which finds its significance exclusively either in the religious experience of the few great individual prophets whose names we know, or in the exact form of their words as they have been reported and transmitted to us. The latter dependence is often unsafe and the former judgement always too narrow. The very existence of a great number of anonymous prophetic oracles and the enormous labours that have been devoted to all the prophetic material by editors and interpreters during a period of up to five hundred years disclose horizons far wider than those we are accustomed to think of as defining the 'prophetic movement' and the 'prophetic period'. The difficulties we encounter in reading these books and in trying to establish the original preaching of the individual prophets are for the most part the direct consequence of the authority which was discerned in their oracles and which invited successive generations to reinterpret them for their own time.

This is the point at which to acknowledge that we do not know exactly how the teaching of the prophets entered the religious tradition of post-exilic Judaism. There is no certain evidence even about the process through which their oracles passed from the spoken to the written word. Jeremiah is the only prophet who is reported to have had a secretary and the account of his activities in Jeremiah 36 sheds more light on the problem than any other single Old Testament passage. The prophet is said to have been commanded by God to take a roll and record all the oracles he had delivered during his ministry of twenty years (v. 2). The purpose of the collection was to provoke the people to repentance at a critical juncture of Judah's history (605 BC), when the threat from Babylon began to loom large (v. 3).

Jeremiah called for the services of Baruch, the scribe, to whom he dictated the prophecies. This is the first explicit reference in the Old Testament to the writing of a *collection* of prophetic oracles, but, we must notice, it provides no proof either that Jeremiah himself could not write, or that he had not recorded any of his oracles on previous occasions. Nor does it necessarily mean that the prophet was changing his method and abandoning direct personal preaching for the written message. This was a special occasion. It was desperately urgent that the people should be warned of the coming disaster and Jeremiah himself was debarred (for some reason unrevealed) from going to the Temple (v. 5). The roll which was dictated personally by the prophet represented, therefore, the credentials of Baruch (vv. 17–18).

As the story is unfolded with great dramatic artistry, we learn how the message was read three times on that fast day in December – to the people (v. 10), to the senior statesmen of Judah (v. 15), and finally, to the king himself (v. 21). Unlike Josiah, his father (see II Kings 22. 11), the king showed no signs of penitence on hearing the word of the Lord (v. 24), but contemptuously slashed the roll with a penknife as it was being read and, bit by bit, threw it into the fire (v. 23). The narrator is at pains to emphasize that God's Word is not thus lightly disposed of and that therefore another roll was written (vv. 27–32).

It is difficult to generalize with confidence about the composition of the prophetic books on the basis of this single account. It is possible, but by no means certain, that Baruch's second roll was the nucleus of the book of Jeremiah as we now have it. It is probable, but again by no means certain, that other prophets were well served by men like Baruch.

It is perhaps not without significance that Jeremiah's roll was first read 'in the chamber of Gemariah the son of Shaphan the secretary' and that Gemariah was among the administrative officials who 'urged the king not to burn the scroll'.[30] It was also in a scribe's chamber that these friendly officials deposited the roll before they went to see the king.[31] Such evidence may well suggest that Baruch's contribution to the preservation of Jeremiah's oracles was no isolated example and that the scribes, who made up the educated section of the community, were responsible for preserving and transmitting the preaching of all the prophets. That the idea of written collections of prophecies was familiar in the sixth century BC is attested by references to the roll which was handed to Ezekiel (to eat!) as a sign of his prophetic commission and to the enormous flying roll in one of the visions of Zechariah, which, it was said, would judge the iniquity of the land.[32]

Whatever the history of their compilation and transmission, we know that the four great prophetic anthologies of Isaiah, Jeremiah, Ezekiel and 'The Twelve' were regarded as authoritative by about 190 BC, when Jesus ben Sira (the author of the book Ecclesiasticus) wrote his roll-call of the heroes of Israel.[33] They are also mentioned by Jesus ben Sira's grandson in the delightful and instructive preface he composed for his translation of Ecclesiasticus from Hebrew into Greek:

Ye are intreated therefore to read with favour and attention, and to pardon us, if in any parts of what we have laboured to interpret, we may seem to fail in some of the phrases. For things originally spoken in Hebrew have not the same force in them, when they are translated into another tongue: and not only these, but *the law itself, and the prophecies, and the*

30. Jer. 36. 10, 25.
31. Jer. 36. 20.
32. Ezek. 2. 8–3. 3; Zech. 5. 1–4; Hab. 2. 2; see pp. 149–52.
33. See pp. 148–9.

rest of the books, have no small difference, when they are spoken in their original language . . . I thought it therefore most necessary for me to apply some diligence and travail to interpret this book; applying indeed much watchfulness and skill in that space of time to bring the book to an end, and set it forth for them also, who in the land of their sojourning are desirous to learn, fashioning their manners beforehand, so as to live according to the law.

This passage from the Apocrypha gives good advice to all who would understand the faith of the prophets. Their oracles were spoken in an unfamiliar idiom and collected in a way which often appears to us quite chaotic. They demand for their understanding, as Ecclesiasticus demanded of its author's grandson, 'some diligence and travail'. It will be fully rewarded if it serves the practical end Jesus ben Sira's grandson had in view.

CHAPTER 3

The Vocation of the Prophets

You cannot go very far in reading the prophetic writings without coming across a passage like the following:

> Thus says the LORD of hosts: 'Do not listen to the words of the prophets who prophesy to you, filling you with vain hopes; they speak visions of their own minds, not from the mouth of the LORD.'[1]

Such a denunciation of the prophets by a prophet is extremely perplexing, until we appreciate that the terms 'prophet' and 'prophesying' have a very wide range of meaning in the Old Testament and so inevitably cover much that illuminates the vocation of men like Amos, Isaiah and Jeremiah, not directly but by contrast.

The feature common to all prophets in the ancient world is that they claimed to speak with the authority of their god. They were essentially *spokesmen*. This basic characteristic is well illustrated by two alternative descriptions of the relationship between Moses and Aaron in the book Exodus. In the first, Aaron is represented as Moses' *spokesman*:

> And you [Moses] shall speak to him and put the words in his mouth; and I will be with your mouth and with his mouth, and will teach you what you shall do. He shall speak for you [Revised Version: He shall be thy *spokesman*] to the people; and he shall be a mouth for you, and you shall be to him as God.[2]

1. Jer. 23. 16.
2. Exod. 4. 15, 16.

In the second description, Aaron is called Moses' *prophet*:

> And the LORD said to Moses, 'See, I make you as God to Pharaoh; and Aaron your brother shall be your prophet. You shall speak all that I command you.'[3]

A prophet was a messenger who spoke on behalf of his god.[4] The term was freely used for those who claimed to speak with the authority of pagan gods – like those with whom Elijah contended on Mount Carmel.[5] It was also employed to describe the institutional prophets of Israel, whose activity and influence were so strongly deprecated by men like Jeremiah. The student of the Old Testament is faced, therefore, with the task of discriminating between the various kinds of prophet and of deciding how much more they have in common than their name and the claim to speak with divine authority which the name implies. This is a delicate undertaking and it has been made more difficult by the work of the editors from whose hands we have received the Hebrew scriptures. In addition to introducing prophets into the historical narratives as mouthpieces of their own sermonizing,[6] they appear to have been largely responsible for giving general currency to the title 'prophet' as a description of men like Amos, Hosea, Isaiah, Micah and Jeremiah, although it is questionable whether they themselves would have acknowledged it.[7] Whether or not any of these great figures ever explicitly repudiated the title depends upon a saying of Amos, of which the interpretation is disputed:

3. Exod. 7. 1, 2.

4. The words with which the prophets introduced their oracles – 'Thus says the LORD' – is an adaptation of the formula used by men employed as messengers in the ancient Near East (cf. Gen. 32. 3–5; 45. 9; Num. 20. 14; 22. 15, 16; I Kgs. 20. 2–5; 22. 27; II Kgs. 19. 1–3; cf. Ezra 1.2). It is even possible that the Hebrew word for prophet (*nābhī*) was originally the ordinary term for a spokesman or messenger, as in one of the Lachish Letters (cf. II Chron. 36. 15, 16).

5. I Kgs. 18. 19.

6. Judg. 6. 7–10; I Sam. 2. 27–36; I Kgs. 13. 1–10; II Kgs. 17. 13.

7. See p. 44.

> Then Amos answered Amaziah, 'I am no prophet, nor one of the sons of the prophets; but I am a herdsman, and a dresser of sycamore trees, and the LORD took me from following the flock, and the LORD said to me, "Go, prophesy to my people Israel." '[8]

It has been suggested that Amos here is not making a solemn pronouncement, but asking an indignant question (as though to say): 'How dare you say that I am not a true prophet because I work with the herds and sycamore trees? Don't you realize that the Lord has called me?' Since the Hebrew text has no verb, some scholars prefer to supply the past tense: 'I *was* no prophet, nor one of the sons of the prophets . . . and the LORD said to me, "Go, prophesy to my people Israel." ' According to this latter view, Amos is claiming that his new status as a prophet rests on a divine call and not on the choice of a profession. He *was* no prophet, because he was not brought up in one of the prophetic schools.[9] It is significant that even those who deny that Amos is explicitly repudiating the title of prophet are bound to recognize that his appeal to an experience of being specially and specifically called by God gives the title a content to which Amaziah, the sanctuary official at Bethel, was wholly unaccustomed. The kind of prophet *he* was used to was the full-time professional who made his living by giving oracles:

> And Amaziah said to Amos, 'O seer, go, flee away to the land of Judah, and eat bread there, and prophesy there; but never again prophesy at Bethel, for it is the king's sanctuary, and it is a temple of the kingdom.'[10]

We are driven to the conclusion that any attempt to characterize the great prophets by defining 'prophecy' in the abstract is foredoomed to failure.

8. Amos 7. 14, 15.
9. See pp. 32–3.
10. Amos 7. 12, 13.

THE INSTITUTIONAL PROPHETS

The institution of prophecy first emerges in Israel at the very beginning of the reign of Saul, who, it is recorded, was instructed by Samuel to go to Gibeah: 'And there, as you come to the city, you will meet a band of prophets coming down from the high place with harp, tambourine, flute, and lyre before them, prophesying. Then the spirit of the Lord will come mightily upon you, and you shall prophesy with them and be turned into another man.'[11] Later, we are told: 'When they came to Gibeah, behold, a band of prophets met him; and the spirit of God came mightily upon him, and he prophesied among them. And when all who knew him before saw how he prophesied with the prophets, the people said to one another, "What has come over the son of Kish? Is Saul also among the prophets?" '[12] A comparable incident is recorded in connection with Saul's search for David after his flight to Ramah:

> Then Saul sent messengers to take David; and when they saw the company of the prophets prophesying, and Samuel standing as head over them, the spirit of God came upon the messengers of Saul, and they also prophesied . . . Then he [Saul] himself went to Ramah . . . and the spirit of God came upon him also, and as he went he prophesied, until he came to Naioth in Ramah. And he too stripped off his clothes, and he too prophesied before Samuel, and lay naked all that day and all that night. Hence it is said, 'Is Saul also among the prophets?'[13]

This evidence suggests that early Israelite prophecy was (*a*) a group phenomenon organized under a leader, (*b*) associated with sanctuaries, (*c*) violently frenzied in character, and (*d*) deliberately stimulated – for example by music. A similar picture emerges from the record of guilds of 'the sons of

11. I Sam. 10. 5, 6.
12. I Sam. 10. 10, 11.
13. I Sam. 19. 20–4.

the prophets' in the ninth century BC. They appear to have been drawn from the more impoverished section of Israelite society[14] and to have lived in communities under the charge of masters like Elisha at such ancient cult centres as Bethel and Jericho.[15] Their predilection for the abnormal and irrational is evident from the fact that Elisha is depicted as a miracle-worker,[16] clairvoyant[17] and, like the prophets encountered by Saul, as using music to stimulate prophetic trance.[18] It comes as no surprise to discover that the 'sons of the prophets' were regarded with contempt as madmen[19] and that the very word 'prophesy' became synonymous with 'raving'.[20]

Although the early prophets were despised, they were also feared and held in superstitious awe.[21] Because they were believed to be in direct contact with God, they were consulted both by individuals on private matters[22] and by the king on matters of public policy, as when Ahab 'gathered the prophets together, about four hundred men, and said to them, "Shall I go to battle against Ramoth-gilead, or shall I forbear?" '[23] The prophets' established institutional role is confirmed by the pagan parallel of 'the four hundred and fifty prophets of Baal and the four hundred prophets of Asherah, who eat at Jezebel's table'.[24]

Although there is little *direct* evidence that the Jerusalem prophets were also organized in guilds in the pre-exilic Temple, it is probable that the post-exilic Chronicler assumed their existence during the period of the monarchy and regarded the guilds of the Temple-singers of his own day as their direct

14. II Kgs. 4. 1–7.
15. II Kgs. 4. 38; 6. 1.
16. See p. 39.
17. II Kgs. 5. 26; 6. 9, 12, 32.
18. II Kgs. 3. 15–20.
19. II Kgs. 9. 11; cf. I Sam. 19. 24.
20. I Kgs. 18. 29.
21. I Kgs. 17. 18; 18. 7; II Kgs. 1. 13.
22. I Kgs. 14. 1–6; II Kgs. 8. 7, 8.
23. I Kgs. 22. 1–40.
24. I Kgs. 18. 19; cf. II Kgs. 10. 19.

successors.[25] Whether or not the Chronicler was correct in his belief, the way in which Micah, Isaiah, Jeremiah and other contemporary sources explicitly associate prophets with the priesthood of Jerusalem leaves us in little doubt that the prophets had an official part in the worship of the Temple.[26]

This view has been strengthened by the recognition in recent years that some of the psalms may contain prophetic oracles, or imply the utterance of them during the performance of the cultic ritual. Psalm 20, for example, was probably composed to accompany a sacrificial offering before the king went out to battle, and the sudden change from intercession for victory (vv. 1–5) to confidence that victory has been guaranteed (vv. 6–9) is best accounted for by supposing that a prophet had intervened in the ritual with an oracle of salvation. This may well have taken a form similar to the oracle in Psalm 21. 8–12, which assures the king that all his foes will be exterminated:

> Your hand will find out all your enemies;
>   your right hand will find out those who hate you.
> You will make them as a blazing oven when you appear.
> The LORD will swallow them up in his wrath;
>   and fire will consume them.
> You will destroy their offspring from the earth,
>   and their children from among the sons of men.
> If they plan evil against you, if they devise mischief,
>   they will not succeed.
> For you will put them to flight; you will aim at their faces
>   with your bows.

Such assurances of victory over the nations, and, therefore, of the king's power to exercise God's universal sovereignty, are a common feature of the royal psalms.[27] Evidence of this kind makes it very probable that oracles against foreign

25. I Chron. 25. 1–8; II Chron. 20. 14–23.
26. Lam. 2. 20; Jer. 23. 11; see pp. 101, 111.
27. Ps. 2. 8, 9; 72. 8–11; 110. 1. 5, 6; cf. 46. 6–10; 47. 8, 9; 48. 4–8.

nations, composed and spoken by institutional prophets, were a significant element during the period of the monarchy in the ceremonies of the Temple.

It has now been established that this prophetic function was recognized by Israel's neighbours in the ancient Near East, to whose practice Israel was almost certainly indebted. Beneath the heavily edited version of the Balaam story in Numbers 22–4, it is still possible, for example, to discern a Mesopotamian prophet, who had been called upon by Balak, king of Moab, to secure victory over Israel: 'Come now, curse this people for me, since they are too mighty for me; perhaps I shall be able to defeat them and drive them from the land; for I know that he whom you bless is blessed, and he whom you curse is cursed.'[28] Discovered in a region not far from that of Balaam, some of the eighteenth-century BC documents from the excavations of the ancient city of Mari incorporate prophetic oracles, which were similarly intended as a preparation for war (against Babylon, among other enemies); and Egyptian execration texts of the same period, consisting of curses against enemies written on pottery before it was ritually smashed, provide a further analogy to Israelite practice. In the light of such evidence, there can be little doubt that the oracle against the foreign nation was one of the earliest forms of prophecy in Israel and that the institutional prophets' fundamental role in society was to secure victory.

It is probable that the book of Nahum affords the best evidence of the activity and outlook of prophets like these. The work is a collection of prophetic liturgies mocking and threatening Nineveh, the capital of Assyria, whose fall to the Babylonians in 612 BC resounded throughout the ancient Near East. The vigour of the language in the core of the book (excluding, that is, the incomplete acrostic psalm of 1. 2–8) is matched, unfortunately, by the vigour of its chauvinism.

Jeremiah's conflict with the institutional prophets of Jerusalem is well documented and revealing. What he primarily repudiated was their ready promise of salvation – 'It shall be

28. Num. 22. 6.

well with you' – and the false optimism of their comfortable words:

> They have healed the wound of my people lightly,
>   saying 'Peace, peace,'
>   when there is no peace.[29]

The fundamental antagonism is dramatically portrayed in the confrontation between Jeremiah and the prophet Hananiah.[30] Jeremiah believed that Babylon was the chosen instrument of God's judgement on his people and had taken a wooden ox-yoke to symbolize his demand for complete submission to the conqueror. This repudiation of prophetic orthodoxy outraged Hananiah, who (as his professional duty required) immediately declared his opposition by breaking the yoke and assuring the people of Babylon's imminent collapse: 'Thus says the LORD: Even so will I break the yoke of Nebuchadnezzar king of Babylon from the neck of all the nations within two years.' Hananiah could claim the whole weight of the Jerusalem tradition to support his declaration, which is why, perhaps, on first hearing it, 'Jeremiah the prophet went his way.'[31]

Although the distinctiveness of the independent prophets was not always fully appreciated by the historians and theologians of Israel, with the consequence that they are sometimes represented as approximating to the institutional model,[32] it says much for the radical character of the central tradition of the Old Testament that it gave prominence to a mere half-dozen or so eccentric laymen over the hundreds of institutional prophets who made a living by their professional services.

29. Jer. 6. 14; 23. 17; cf. 14. 13–16.
30. Jer. 27. 1–28. 17.
31. Jer. 28. 10, 11.
32. II Kgs. 19. 1–7; 20. 1–11; Jer. 13. 1–11; 28. 1–8; 43. 8–13. Their distinctiveness is similarly blurred by the company they have been made to keep in the prophetic scriptures.

It is obvious that the prophets who acted as professional consultants must have been proficient in some kind of technique for 'discovering' the will of God and it is equally clear that their methods associate them very closely with the old cultic religion of Canaan. Of these methods, perhaps the most naively mechanical were the various forms of divination and casting the sacred lot. The latter is well illustrated by Saul's use of 'Urim and Thummim' to get an answer from God: 'O LORD God of Israel, why hast thou not answered thy servant this day? If this guilt is in me or in Jonathan my son, O LORD God of Israel, give *Urim*; but if this guilt is in thy people Israel, give *Thummin*.'[33]

Nobody is quite sure what exactly this device was, but it is probable that marked stones were used, of which the interpretation was settled beforehand, as when we toss a coin. We need go no further than the evidence supplied by the Old Testament itself to recognize that divination, so far from being peculiar to the Hebrews, was a favourite pagan method of obtaining a divine ruling.[34] It is not surprising, therefore, that men like Micah and Jeremiah should have vehemently opposed the prophets who practised divination and that there should be ancient laws in line with the prophets' protest.[35]

Human beings have always been susceptible to communications represented as having been received in a state of ecstatic trance. Many bogus types of 'spiritualism' exploit our credulity even today, very much as the institutional prophets of Israel (literally) 'cashed in' on the gullibility of their contemporaries in the eighth and seventh centuries BC. A scathing comment from Isaiah on the prophets who 'err in vision' through wine and strong drink suggests one possible source of their inspiration.[36] Another stimulus was

33. I Sam. 14. 41; cf. I Sam. 23. 9–12; 28. 6; 30. 7, 8; Ezek. 13. 6, 7; Deut. 33. 8; Num. 27. 21.
34. Num. 22. 7; I Sam. 6. 2; Isa. 44. 25; 47. 12, 13; Ezek. 21. 21.
35. Mic. 3. 11; Jer. 14. 14; 27. 9; 29. 8; Isa. 3. 2, 3; Ezek. 13. 6, 7, 23; Zech. 10. 2; I Sam. 15. 23; 28. 3; II Kgs. 17. 17; 21. 6; Deut. 18. 10; Lev. 19. 26; 20. 6, 27.
36. Isa. 28. 7; cf. Mic. 2. 11.

music, which, it seems, both induced and controlled 'spirit-possession'.[37] Saul, as we have seen, is told that he will 'meet a band of prophets coming down from the high place with harp, tambourine, flute, and lyre before them, prophesying. Then the spirit of the LORD will come mightily upon you, and you shall prophesy with them and be turned into another man.'[38] It is hardly surprising that prophecy could be regarded as being synonymous with lunacy.[39] Evidently, there were prophets in Israel whose behaviour was not dissimilar to the frantic raving of Jezebel's prophets of Baal, who 'cried aloud, and cut themselves after their custom with swords and lances, until the blood gushed out upon them. And as midday passed, they raved on until the time of the offering of the oblation, but there was no voice; no one answered, no one heeded.'[40] The independent prophets are never found employing artificial stimuli and, in the pre-exilic period, they even avoided attributing their oracles to the 'spirit of God'.[41] They chose, instead, to describe their 'inspiration' in less ambiguous terms, as when they speak of experiencing 'the hand of the LORD'.[42]

Dreams represent another of the media by which the institutional prophets claimed to receive divine intelligence. Jeremiah makes it quite clear that he has no use for them:

I have heard what the prophets have said who prophesy lies in my name, saying, 'I have dreamed, I have dreamed!' How long shall there be lies in the heart of the prophets who prophesy lies, and who prophesy the deceit of their own heart, who think to make my people forget my name by their dreams which they tell one another, even as their fathers forgot my

37. I Sam. 16. 14–23; 18. 10, 11; 19. 9. cf. II Kgs. 3. 15; I Chron. 25. 1, 2; Exod. 15. 20, 21.
38. I Sam. 10. 5, 6.
39. Jer. 29. 26; Hos. 9. 7; I Sam. 19. 23, 24; cf. II Kgs. 9. 11; Zech. 13. 1–6.
40. I Kgs. 18. 28, 29; cf. Zech. 13. 6.
41. Mic. 3. 8 probably reflects a post-exilic outlook; cf. Num. 11. 29; Joel 2. 28; Ezek. 11. 5; Isa. 61. 1; II Chron. 20. 14, 15; 24. 20.
42. Isa. 8. 11; cf. Ezek. 1. 3; 3. 14; 8. 1; 37. 1; I Kgs. 18. 46.

name for Baal? Let the prophet who has a dream tell the dream, but let him who has my word speak my word faithfully. What has *straw* in common with *wheat?* says the LORD.[43]

Straw and wheat is an admirable summary of the relationship between the institutional prophets and Israel's great men of God. This does not mean, however, that the independent prophets were (as once was thought) isolated individual geniuses detached from the mainstream of Israel's religious life. The content of their message proves beyond any doubt that they were reinterpreting the tradition of faith which stemmed from the age of Moses. It is, therefore, in this direction that we must seek their historical antecedents.

The books of Kings contain a collection of stories,[44] which, if they cannot be said to bridge the gap between Moses and Amos, at least establish the existence (about 850 BC) of what has been wittily labelled *Mosaic*, as distinct from *Amos*aic, prophecy.[45] The dominant figure of these stories is the prophet Elijah. All we know about him has been preserved in a popular tradition, of which, presumably, his successor Elisha may be taken as being fairly representative. The prophetic communities – the 'sons of the prophets' – over which Elisha presided[46] are probably responsible for claiming for their master a 'double share' of Elijah's spirit[47] and what that meant for them is clear from the miracle-working they have ascribed to him.[48] Although their love of the miraculous has also coloured the accounts of Elijah,[49] he emerges, nevertheless, as a gaunt desert figure of forbidding appearance and

---

43. Jer. 23. 25–8; cf. 27. 9; 29. 8; Zech. 10. 2; Deut. 13. 1–3.
44. The stories of Elijah: I Kgs. 17–19; 21; II Kgs. 1–2; the stories of Elisha: I Kgs. 19. 19–21; II Kgs. 2–7; 8. 1–15; 9. 1–13; 13. 14–21.
45. Notice the references to the 'prophets of the Lord'; I Kgs. 18. 4, 22; 19. 10.
46. II Kgs. 2. 3, 5; 4. 1, 38; 6. 1–4; 9. 1; see p. 33.
47. II Kgs. 2. 9.
48. II Kgs. 2. 19–22, 23–5; 4. 1–7, 11–37, 38–41; 6. 4–7; 13. 14–19.
49. I Kgs. 17. 8–16, 17–24; 19. 5–8.

fierce conviction[50] – a worthy successor to Moses and a convincing forerunner of Amos. Although none of his oracles has been preserved, this 'Troubler of Israel'[51] had clearly stood in the Council of God[52] and heard his word.[53] His prophetic zeal symbolizes and expresses the distinctiveness of Israel's faith:

> I have been very jealous for the LORD the God of hosts; for the people of Israel have forsaken thy covenant, thrown down thy altars, and slain they prophets with the sword; and I, even I only, am left; and they seek my life, to take it away.[54]

In the ninth century BC, the faith of Israel was seriously imperilled by the old Canaanite religion of Palestine,[55] fortified, as it was, in Ahab's reign (about 869–850 BC) by the establishment of a Baal cult at the behest of the Tyrian Jezebel, his domineering wife.[56] It was in this critical situation that Israel's Mosaic tradition found in a new kind of prophecy its appropriate mode of expression.

Three episodes recorded of the ministry of Elijah illustrate the character of this momentous development. In the scene on Mount Carmel,[57] Elijah in splendid isolation exposes the fraudulence of the Canaanite gods and their raving prophets and makes an uncompromising demand for a decision between the God of Israel and Baal:

> 'How long will you go limping with two different opinions? If the LORD is God, follow him; but if Baal, then follow him.' And the people did not answer him a word.[58]

50. II Kgs. 1. 8; I Kgs. 18. 46.
51. I Kgs. 18. 17; cf. 21. 20.
52. I Kgs. 17. 1; 18. 15; see pp. 47–8.
53. I Kgs. 17. 2, 8; 18. 36; 19. 9; II Kgs. 10. 17.
54. I Kgs. 19. 10.
55. I Kgs. 18. 17–19; II Kgs. 1. 2, 3; see pp. 104–5.
56. I Kgs. 16. 29–33.
57. I Kgs. 18. 20–40.
58. I Kgs. 18. 21.

The scene on Mount Horeb goes further. Elijah had confronted Baal; now he is confronted by the God of Israel.[59] Through a profound spiritual experience, Elijah learns that prophecy is not a matter of using word and action to call down divine power, but rather, a matter of responding in word and action to God's own self-disclosure:

> And behold, the LORD passed by, and a great and strong wind rent the mountains, and broke in pieces the rocks before the LORD, but the LORD was not in the wind; and after the wind an earthquake, but the LORD was not in the earthquake; and after the earthquake a fire, but the LORD was not in the fire; and after the fire a still small voice. And when Elijah heard it, he wrapped his face in his mantle and went out and stood at the entrance of the cave.[60]

The God who discloses himself to Elijah is none other than the God of Moses; we are clearly intended to recognize the significance of the Mount of Revelation.[61]

In the scene at Jezreel, Elijah demonstrates prophecy's new maturity.[62] His impassioned defence of the right of a private citizen to withstand the rapacity of a despotic king is universal in its appeal. In its own time and situation, however, it illustrates the head-on clash between Israel's traditional social order and the new society introduced by the monarchy, which was only another side of the religious conflict dramatized on Mount Carmel. Elijah's denunciation of Ahab for acquiescing in Naboth's murder in order to confiscate his family property is an authentic response to the 'still small voice' of prophetic revelation and is echoed by more than one prophet in the following centuries.[63]

59. I Kgs. 19. 1–18.
60. I Kgs. 19. 11–13.
61. Exod. 3. 1–6; 19. 16–25; 33. 17–23.
62. I Kgs. 21. 1–20.
63. Mic. 2. 1–5; Isa. 5. 8–10.

THE INDEPENDENT PROPHETS

The recent recognition of the importance of institutional prophecy throughout the period of the monarchy has made the relationship to it of prophets like Amos, Hosea, Micah, Isaiah and Jeremiah a much-debated question. Two main views have been taken. The first concentrates on the fact that these radical teachers of the eighth and seventh centuries BC were called prophets like their anonymous contemporaries and are represented as sharing in some degree their experience, their role and their methods. From these considerations, the conclusion has been drawn that it is wrong to make a sharp distinction between the two types of prophet, as though one were 'true' and the other 'false', and necessary to suppose that they were engaged in a common task, even to the extent of collaborating in the cult of the sanctuaries.

A second and very different view is possible. We may insist that it is misleading to give too much weight to the title 'prophet' and to concentrate on the common *external* features with which the title is associated, since these do not go to the heart of the matter and, in any case, were almost certainly exaggerated in the tradition which preserved and shaped the prophetic books. The conclusion to which we may be led is that Amos and his successors were even more distinctive than they are now represented as being and that they cannot be adequately understood as a variety, even a rare variety, of prophecy as an institutional phenomenon.

We may approach the current debate by setting down a number of considerations which are not generally disputed. (1) The independent prophets are nowhere depicted as being members of prophetic guilds; they are figures who stand alone. (2) The independent prophets were remembered for what they said rather than for what they did; only from them has a body of teaching been preserved. (3) The independent prophets were not specialist consultants, who were paid for their services; characteristically, they take the initiative in proclaiming their message, without waiting to be asked. (4) The independent prophets were not workers of miracles; the healing of Hezekiah and the miraculous reversing of the sun ascribed to Isaiah come from a highly legendary source,[64] and, in providing the exception, prove the rule. (5) The independent prophets did not practise clairvoyance; their oracles concerning the future were not detailed predictions arising out of any special faculty of foresight, but, rather, proclamations of what was morally certain on the basis of their spiritual insight. (6) The independent prophets did not employ artificial stimuli (like music) or techniques of divination (like dreams) to achieve their oracular utterances; they spoke because they could not remain silent. (7) The independent prophets did not ascribe their experience or activity to spirit-possession; the variety of the literary forms they employ, the individuality of their style and the coherence of their message exclude the possibility that they proclaimed their oracles in a state of irrational frenzy. (8) The independent prophets were fully aware of the activities of the institutional prophets and were vehemently opposed to them.[65] (9) At least two, and probably three, of the pre-exilic independent prophets proclaimed the destruction of Jerusalem and its Temple,[66] and all five of them were vehemently critical of the sacrificial worship of the sanctuaries.[67] The institutional prophets, on the other hand, played an official part in the cult. (10) The independent prophets were characteristically prophets of judgement, whereas the institutional prophets were exclusively prophets of salvation.

These ten points of difference strongly suggest that there was a deep gulf between the two types of 'prophet', but a number of counter-arguments are regularly advanced and these must be considered.

(1) The strongest argument for affirming a close relationship between the independent and institutional prophets is that they are called by the same name; both are said to

64. II Kgs. 20. 1–11.
65. Jer. 23. 9–32; 29. 24–32; Mic. 3. 5–12.
66. Mic. 3. 9–12; Jer. 7. 1–15; 26. 1–16; Isa. 29. 1–8.
67. See pp. 68–72.

prophesy. Thus we read: 'Then the *prophet* Jeremiah spoke to Hananiah the *prophet* . . . "The prophets who preceded you *and me* from ancient times prophesied war, famine, and pestilence against many countries and great kingdoms".'[68] Since Hananiah is clearly an institutional prophet, the association of the two types, it seems, could hardly be closer. Against this, however, must be set a number of significant facts: (*a*) the overwhelming majority of the references to 'prophets' and 'prophesying' in the Old Testament describe institutional prophets; (*b*) the description of the independent figures as 'prophets' appears to be confined to material which shows the influence of the work of editors after 587 BC,[69] and more particularly the deuteronomists;[70] (*c*) the independent prophets are never recorded as describing themselves as 'prophets', except, by implication, Isaiah, who refers to his wife as 'the prophetess'.[71] Amos quite explicitly denies that he was a prophet or one of 'the sons of the prophets', although he is compelled to use the verb 'prophesy' to describe his work as God's spokesman to the people.[72]

In the light of this evidence, it is difficult to avoid the conclusion that the use in our sources of the words 'prophets' and 'prophesy' for both institutional and independent prophets is far less significant in determining their relationship than at first appears. Indeed, it may mainly indicate that the writers of the deuteronomic school had approximated the two types in the interest of their comprehensive theory that God was sovereign and active throughout Israel's history by sending 'his servants the prophets'.[73] The prophets who play so large a part in I and II Kings are certainly a curious conflation of the institutional and independent types and it is possible that we are primarily indebted to the deuteronomic

68. Jer. 28. 5–8.
69. Isa. 37. 2; 38. 1; 39. 3; Jer. 1. 5; 19. 14; 20. 2; 25. 13; 29. 1; 45. 1; 46. 1; 47. 1.
70. Jer. 26. 4–6; 29. 19; 35. 15; 44. 4; Amos 3. 7.
71. Isa. 8. 3.
72. See pp. 30–1.
73. II Kgs. 9. 7; 17. 13, 23; 21. 10; 24. 2; cf. Jer. 7. 25, 26; 26. 5; 35. 15.

historian for the once popular and still prevalent notion that all Israel's prophets belonged to a single and developing tradition.

(2) One of the most obvious features in common between the institutional and independent prophet is the use of so-called *symbolic actions*. Just as the institutional prophet Zedekiah 'made for himself horns of iron, and said, "Thus says the Lord, 'With these you shall push the Syrians until they are destroyed' " '[74] and Elisha on his death-bed 'laid his hands upon the king's hands' before he shot the arrows and struck the ground with them,[75] so also the independent prophets are recorded as having performed strange and significant acts. Isaiah, it is said, went about Jerusalem for three years stripped like a prisoner of war, as a warning that Egypt would be conquered by the Assyrians and was, therefore, useless as Judah's ally.[76] Jeremiah was commanded to go to one of the gates of Jerusalem and deliberately break a bottle, as a sign that the idolatrous city would be irreparably smashed,[77] and, on another occasion, to wear an ox-yoke as a sign that Judah must accept the yoke of Babylon.[78]

It is clear that all these symbolic actions are similar in form and that they are related to primitive acts of imitative magic, which in the ancient Near East (as elsewhere) were held actually to bring about the situation they depicted. Technically, the prophetic examples are not magical, because God is not coerced by the acts but, rather, is their originator; he commands the prophets to undertake them and, like his words, they are the expression of his purpose. Nevertheless, the symbolic actions of the institutional prophets were not far removed from the realm of magic, since they were evidently expected to effect a change in the situation.

It is often asserted that the similar acts of the independent prophets were performed with a similar intention. While it is

74. I Kgs. 22. 11.
75. II Kgs. 13. 14–19.
76. Isa. 20. 1–6.
77. Jer. 19. 1–15.
78. Jer. 27. 1–28. 17; cf. 13. 1–11; 43. 8–13; 51. 59–64.

impossible to prove the contrary, it is probable that the similarity is superficial and has been greatly exaggerated. The acts of the independent prophets have the appearance of being genuinely symbolic, rather than in any sense magical; they are always public demonstrations that declare God's purpose to his people, on the principle that actions speak louder than words, and are always intended to elicit a rational response.[79] They are, moreover, relatively rare in the records of the independent prophets and some of them look like legends that originated in later popular tradition.[80]

The book of Ezekiel, which in so many ways is a good witness to later popular tradition, abounds in examples of prophetic symbolism,[81] but it explicitly presents them as being simply a method of teaching.[82] We may conclude, therefore, that the evidence of symbolic actions does nothing to narrow the gap between institutional and independent prophecy.

(3) The independent prophets, it is claimed, resembled the institutional prophets in the *abnormality of their experience*; they too lost control of their faculties and received their divine revelations in a state of frenzy. For lack of any decisive evidence of the independent prophets' inner experience, opinion on this subject is likely to remain divided. The account we have of their 'calls' to become God's spokesmen are all characterized by a sense of responsibility which totally excludes the idea that they were beside themselves in any kind of abnormal state.[83] Their visions, too, are sober and restrained[84] and presuppose a continuous, personal and intelligent knowledge of God. This is not to deny, however, that the religious experience of the great independent prophets was quite out of the ordinary, as the agonized 'confessions' of Jeremiah make perfectly plain.[85]

---

79. Jer. 5. 12–14; 32. 1–15.
80. Jer. 13. 1–11; 43. 8–13; 51. 59–64.
81. Ezek. 4. 1–17; 5. 1–17; 12. 1–20; 24. 15–27; 37. 15–23.
82. Ezek. 24. 19; 37. 18.
83. Amos 7. 14, 15; Isa. 6. 1–13; Jer. 1. 4–10.
84. Amos 7. 1–8. 3; Jer. 1. 11, 12; see pp. 49–50.
85. Jer. 15. 10–21; 20. 7–18; cf. 4. 19; 5. 14; 6. 11; 23. 29.

Extraordinary religious experience, as a remarkable passage in the book of Numbers recognizes, may, however, be of very different kinds: 'If there is a prophet among you, I the Lord make myself known to him in a vision, I speak with him in a dream. Not so with my servant Moses; he is entrusted with all my house. With him I speak mouth to mouth, clearly, and not in dark speech; and he beholds the form of the Lord.'[86] To this we may add a comparable description: 'Thus the Lord used to speak to Moses face to face, as a man speaks to his friend.'[87]

The independent prophets of Israel stand in the tradition of Moses; like him, they were men who had been admitted to God's intimate circle and taken into his confidence.[88] Jeremiah is the most explicit of the prophets in affirming that such direct personal knowledge of God is the fundamental ground of true prophetic authority. He sums up his conviction in a splendidly suggestive word (*ṣôdh*), which is translated 'council', in his diagnosis of the failure of the professional prophets:

> For who among them has stood in
> the council of the LORD
> to perceive and to hear his word,
> or who has given heed to his word
> and listened?
>
> I did not send the prophets,
> yet they ran;
> I did not speak to them,
> yet they prophesied.
>
> But if they had stood in my council,
> then they would have proclaimed
> my words to my people,

86. Num. 12. 6–8.
87. Exod. 33. 11; cf. Wisd. 7. 27.
88. Deut. 18. 15; 34. 10; Hos. 12. 13.

and they would have turned them
from their evil way,
and from the evil of their doings.[89]

The significance of the word *ṣôdh* may be judged from the other Old Testament passages in which it is used. We find that it means, for instance, a group of friends who enjoy each other's company and (as the Psalmist puts it) take 'sweet counsel' together.[90] It is also used of the secrets of intimate acquaintances, or of conspirators, who are as 'thick as thieves';[91] and, most significantly, it describes God's 'covenant-friendship' with his servants:

The friendship [*ṣôdh*] of the LORD is for
those who fear him,
and he makes known to them his covenant.[92]

The prophets had been admitted into the privileged circle of God's Heavenly Council – a concept derived from the royal courts of the ancient Near East.[93] For this reason, they were able to hear and proclaim the counsel of the Lord:

Surely the Lord GOD does nothing,
without revealing his secret [*ṣôdh*]
to his servants the prophets.[94]

It must always be something of an impertinence to attempt to stretch any sort of spiritual experience on the rack of our psychological categories and this is even more obviously true in the case of the great prophets, of whose inner consciousness our evidence is no less slight than our ability to interpret it. The significant discovery we make as we read the prophetic

89. Jer. 23. 18, 21, 22; cf. Job 15. 8; Ezek. 13. 9.
90. Ps. 55. 14; cf. Jer. 6. 11; 15. 17; Gen. 49. 6; Job 19. 19.
91. Prov. 11. 13; 15. 22; 20. 19; 25. 9; Ps. 64. 2; 83. 3.
92. Ps. 25. 14; cf. Prov. 3. 32; Job 29. 4.
93. Job 1. 1–2. 13; 15. 8. Ps. 82; 89. 7; I Kgs. 22. 19–22.
94. Amos 3. 7; cf. Isa. 6. 8.

writings is that the really great men of God did not wear their heart on their sleeve for all to examine. They leave preoccupation with the externals of religion to lesser mortals. Like all the Hebrews, they knew nothing of our dubious distinction between 'subjective' and 'objective' experience, just as we know little of their ability to embrace the material and spiritual worlds in a profound unity, so that mundane physical experience could become vibrant with spiritual significance. This meant that the everyday life of the prophets was always potentially a manifestation of God's will and that very little was needed to strike them into making specific utterances.[95] For example, in the first chapter of Jeremiah, we read:

> And the word of the LORD came to me, saying, 'Jeremiah, what do you see?' And I said, 'I see a rod of *almond*.' Then the LORD said to me, 'You have seen well, for I am *watching* over my word to perform it.'[96]

As the marginal reading in our translations indicates, the words italicized represent two very similar Hebrew words – *shāqēdh* (almond) and *shōqēdh* (watching). The sight of an almond tree and the sound of its name brought to articulate expression the prophet's knowledge of God's 'wakefulness'. Similarly, when Amos saw a basket of summer fruit, the word for summer (*qáyiç*) released his prophetic conviction that Israel was doomed and approaching its end (*qēç*).[97] The apparent triviality of this chance association is in startling contrast with the elaborate devices employed by the institutional prophets when they wished to obtain an oracle.

Just as the great prophets did not differentiate between spiritual and physical experience, so they did not separate what we should call their religious and their moral experience. The concern of the prophets with moral issues would lead us

---

95. See Jer. 1. 13, 14 (the boiling cauldron); 18. 1–4 (the potter); 24. 1–3 (the two baskets of figs).
96. Jer. 1. 11, 12.
97. Amos 8. 1, 2.

to expect that an. urge to prophesy often arose from the demands of their conscience. If we are looking for external features in terms of which we may explain the authority of the prophets, the significance of their moral discrimination will escape us. If, however, we acknowledge that conscience is one of the ways of knowing God, we shall attach the greatest importance to the hint given in Jeremiah:

> Therefore thus says the LORD:
> 'If you return, I will restore you,
> and you shall stand before me.
> If you utter what is precious, and
> not what is worthless,
> you shall be as my mouth.'[98]

Here the prophet is called upon to acknowledge his own defection from God and repent of his self-pity. Only by the discrimination which flows from a heightened personal awareness can he discharge his prophetic office. Again, we notice the gulf which separates the corybantic seer and the true man of God.

If the inner core of the prophetic consciousness is this intensified spiritual and moral awareness, we must expect to fail in all our clumsy attempts to split up into their constituent elements the visionary experiences the prophets record. Their simple introductions – 'Thus the Lord GOD showed me,' 'I saw the Lord,' and 'Jeremiah, what do you see?'[99] – suggest a continuous, personal and intelligent knowledge of God, very different from both the pathological frenzy of some of the institutional prophets and the stylized visions of (say) Zechariah, which, without the services of an interpreting angel, are enigmatic 'dark speeches'.[100]

There is always a danger of our being tempted to degrade the consciousness of the prophets to the impersonal level, in order (as we falsely suppose) to safeguard the objective

98. Jer. 15. 19.
99. Amos. 7. 1, 4, 7; 8. 1; Isa. 6. 1; Jer. 1. 11.
100. Zech. 1. 9, 19; cf. Ezek. 40. 3, 4; see p. 159.

authority of their oracles. That such an insensitive proce-
dure is unnecessary is well demonstrated by the fragments
we possess of Jeremiah's spiritual diary. It contains one of
the most shattering passages in the Bible:

> Cursed be the day
>   on which I was born!
> The day when my mother bore me,
>   let it not be blessed!
> Cursed be the man
>   who brought the news to my father,
> 'A son is born to you,'
>   making him very glad.
> Let that man be like the cities
>   which the LORD overthrew without pity;
> let him hear a cry in the morning
>   and an alarm at noon,
> because he did not kill me in the womb;
>   so my mother would have been my grave,
>   and her womb for ever great.
> Why did I come forth from the womb
>   to see toil and sorrow,
>   and spend my days in shame?[101]

This terrible cry of dereliction is not a denial of the prophet's
vocation, but the very strongest confirmation of its depth.
Jeremiah had accepted the office of being God's spokesman
to the nation, but not only that; he had also undertaken to
bear in his own life the burden of God's grief at his people's
sin. Hosea before him had suffered the conflict between the
love which must express itself in judgement and the love
which demands mercy, and had boldly identified his own
pathos with the pathos of God himself:

> How can I give you up, O Ephraim!
> How can I hand you over, O Israel!

---

101. Jer. 20. 14–18; cf. Job 3. 1–26.

My heart recoils within me,
   my compassion grows warm and tender.[102]

A large part of Jeremiah's spiritual anguish sprang from his recognition that he himself was failing in his response to God. There were occasions when he became conscience-stricken with the fear that the zeal of his denunciations had outstripped in austerity the righteous love of God for his people.[103] And there were times when his human sympathy pleaded for pity and almost persuaded him to give in and relinquish his mission. A teacher of human wisdom may decide to retire, but not so a prophet:

If I say, 'I will not mention him,
   or speak any more in his name,'
there is in my heart as it were a burning fire
   shut up in my bones,
and I am weary with holding it in,
   and I cannot.[104]

It was of this same moral and spiritual compulsion that Amos spoke in one of the few hints he has left us of his inner sense of vocation: 'The Lord GOD has spoken; who can but prophesy?'[105]

Jeremiah proved the intense reality of his prophetic vocation by faithfulness not only in private spiritual agony, but also in a public life of isolation and persecution. His divine commission won for him the hostility of his family and the ostracism of his familiar friends and it meant sacrificing the possibility of marriage and a happy family life.[106] The friendship of God was indeed a costly privilege:

102. Hos. 11. 8.
103. Jer. 17. 14–18.
104. Jer. 20. 9; cf. 5. 14; 6. 11.
105. Amos 3. 8; cf. Isa. 8. 11; Ezek. 3. 14.
106. Jer. 16. 1, 2; 15. 10–21; 18. 18–23; 20. 1–6; 26. 7–19; 32. 2–5; 36. 5; 37. 16–21; 38. 1–13.

But I was like a gentle lamb
  led to the slaughter.
I did not know it was against me
  they devised schemes, saying,
'Let us destroy the tree with its fruit,
  let us cut him off from the land of the living,
  that his name be remembered no more.'[107]

We are inevitably reminded of the Servant of the Lord in Second Isaiah, whose experience corresponded so closely to that of Jeremiah that some scholars have found in the likeness a clue to the baffling problem of the Servant's identity:

He was oppressed, and he was afflicted,
  yet he opened not his mouth;
like a lamb that is led to the slaughter,
  and like a sheep that before its shearers is dumb,
  so he opened not his mouth.[108]

The outstanding feature in this recorded experience is its personal dedication. Here is the proof, if proof be needed, that the great prophets were servants in God's household and not mere tools in his hand. Their personalities were neither dissolved by fusion with the divine in any sort of 'mystic union', nor yet swept aside by the violence of any non-moral ecstatic afflatus.[109] When they were commissioned as 'men of God', they remained *men* – and that is why they can so powerfully mediate to us the self-disclosure of the personal God. If, then, we wish to speak of the compelling power of God with which the prophetic oracles surge, we must remember that it was the deepest kind of compulsion – that which is known in personal communion and grounded in moral conviction.

107. Jer. 11. 19.
108. Isa. 53. 7; see pp. 123–4.
109. The point is well illustrated by Jer. 42. 7, which suggests that the prophet meditated for no less than ten days before speaking in God's name. A similar interval is indicated in Jer. 28. 11, 12.

This conclusion about the source of the astonishing urgency of the prophets' teaching is confirmed by the accounts they have left us of their 'calls' to the prophetic ministry.[110] Significantly, they are usually cast in the form of a dialogue with God in which it is he who takes the initiative.

These men were not born to a profession; they did not pass through a novitiate or join any prophetic guild; nor did they submit themselves to a course of theological instruction. They finished as they began – laymen. Amos (like Elisha) was working in the fields when the 'call' came: 'The LORD took me from following the flock, and the LORD said to me, "Go, prophesy to my people Israel." '[111] The simplicity of this statement is self-authenticating. Moses, similarly, was tending his father-in-law's flock when he saw the vision in the Burning Bush; the account of it in Exodus corresponds closely in form to that of Isaiah, although the latter received his call in the Temple.[112] Jeremiah and the Servant of the Lord in Second Isaiah expressed both the certainty they felt about their vocation and their recognition of its irregularity by formal, institutional criteria, by describing it as a mission to which they were destined before birth:

> Before I formed you in the womb I knew you,
> and before you were born I consecrated you;
> I appointed you a prophet to the nations.[113]

Incredulity and a feeling of incapacity appear to have been the common human reaction to God's communication of his purpose. The exquisite confession of Jeremiah – 'Ah, Lord GOD! Behold, I do not know how to speak, for I am only a youth' – is echoed in the words attributed to Moses:

110. Amos 7. 14, 15; Isa. 6; Jer. 1. 4–10; Ezek. 1. 1–3. 27; Exod. 3–4; I Sam. 3; cf. Isa. 42. 1–4; 49. 1–6.
111. Amos 7. 15; I Kgs. 19. 19–21; cf. II Sam. 7. 8, 9.
112. Exod. 3. 1–6; Isa. 6. 1–9.
113. Jer. 1. 5; cf. Isa. 49. 1, 5.

Oh, my Lord, I am not eloquent, either heretofore or since thou hast spoken to thy servant; but I am slow of speech and of tongue.[114]

How very different this is from the brazen confidence of the professional prophet! The drama of Isaiah's vision develops rather differently. Israel's desperate need of the prophetic message is first made plain by a contrast between the abundant worth of God (his 'glory') and the wretched unworthiness of his people as represented by Isaiah himself. This contrast so penetrated the prophet's innermost being that it provoked the classic confession:

Woe is me! For I am lost; for I am a man of unclean lips, and I dwell in the midst of a people of unclean lips; for my eyes have seen the King, the LORD of hosts![115]

In each case, God makes a demand which is insupportable without his succour. Therefore a promise of his presence follows:

But I will be with you ... Now therefore go, and I will be with your mouth and teach you what you shall speak.[116]

In all these accounts, there is the explicit recognition that the prophet's mission will be accomplished only in the teeth of powerful opposition. This may even deny the prophet's authority:

Then Moses answered, 'But behold, they will not believe me or listen to my voice, for they will say, "The LORD did not appear to you." '[117]

Nevertheless, the message must be proclaimed – 'whether they

114. Exod. 4. 10; cf. Jer. 1. 6; Exod. 6. 12; Judg. 6. 15.
115. Isa. 6. 5; compare the vision of Ezek. 1. 4–28.
116. Exod. 3. 12 and 4. 12; cf. Isa. 6. 6–8; Jer. 1. 9; 15. 19.
117. Exod. 4. 1; cf. Jer. 1. 8; I Sam. 3. 11; Ezek. 3. 4–9.

hear, or refuse to hear';[118] that it might ultimately fail to awaken a response is reflected – with that lack of discrimination between purpose and result so characteristic of Hebrew thought and so perplexing to us[119] – in the conclusion of Isaiah's initial vision. The prophet is commissioned (apparently) only to confirm the nation in its moral and spiritual lethargy:

And he said, 'Go, and say to this people:
"Hear and hear, but do not understand;
see and see, but do not perceive."
Make the heart of this people fat,
and their ears heavy,
and shut their eyes;
lest they see with their eyes,
and hear with their ears,
and understand with their hearts,
and turn and be healed.'[120]

Again, we notice what a difference there is between this moral seriousness and the easy optimism of the institutional prophet.

We cannot penetrate further than these confessions take us into the secret of the utter conviction which informs the life and preaching of all the great prophets. Their knowledge of God was too deep and personal to be compatible with any kind of religiosity. It is therefore not surprising that they describe their initial and vital religious experience in the modest form of a conversation with God in the context of their everyday pursuits. It was enough for them that God spoke to them through the life with which they were familiar, by giving it a new dimension – that of himself, his love and his righteousness. This new dimension disclosed the divine purpose; and that compelled their utterance.

118. Ezek. 2. 7.
119. See, for example, Hos. 8. 4; Hab. 2. 10; Isa. 30. 1; 44. 9; Jer. 7. 18.
120. Isa. 6. 9, 10.

CHAPTER 4

The Preaching of the Prophets

The Hebrews, like most other ancient peoples, were quite incapable of appreciating abstract ideas. Beneath most of the nouns of the Old Testament, there throbs a living verb. One might almost say that Hebrew religion is a religion of the verb rather than the noun, because it finds its characteristic expression in *action*. This illuminates its moral strength and the fact that the self-disclosure of God in the Old Testament is given in the history of the life of a people and not in a series of doctrinal propositions.

From the very beginning, the Israelites conceived of God as a personal being, whom they described in a riot of metaphor – and on such a scale that it is possible to build up an almost complete picture of Hebrew society from the images they put to theological use. Christians have become so accustomed to a small selection of these metaphors (such as King and Judge), that they have tended to interpret them too literally and use them as something like 'verbal photographs'. It is easy to forget that they belong, not to the world of exact representation or precise definition, but to the world of poetic imagination – a world in which language is treated with such splendid impropriety that the little hills rejoice and the valleys laugh and sing.[1]

Many of our best popular hymns have their roots in this rich soil of poetic awareness. They can, therefore, prepare us to recapture something of the world from which the prophets speak. For example, the familiar hymn of John Newton, which begins 'How sweet the name of Jesus sounds', conveys a meaning that is clear enough, while at the same time absolutely forbidding a prosaic and pedestrian interpretation:

1. Ps. 65. 12, 13.

> Jesus! my Shepherd, Husband, Friend,
>> My Prophet, Priest, and King.
> My Lord, my Life, my Way, my End,
>> Accept the praise I bring.

It is when, as in this verse, metaphors are mixed with so careless a rapture, that we learn to understand the (limited) contribution of each one of them in its proper poetic context. We must approach most of the poetic oracles of the prophets in exactly the same way.

No Old Testament writer paused to refine his language before speaking of God. That is why every page of the Hebrew scriptures abounds in imagery, which (to our literalistic Western minds) is quite bewildering. For example, God's relationship to his people is represented under the figures of a father,[2] mother,[3] brother,[4] husband,[5] friend,[6] warrior,[7] shepherd,[8] farmer,[9] metal-worker,[10] builder,[11] potter,[12] fuller,[13] physician,[14] judge,[15] water-seller,[16] king,[17] and scribe[18] – to mention, almost at random, a few of the relationships and activities of the people's common life. The relative rarity of impersonal metaphors distinguishes the God of Israel from the gods of the nations, who are regularly likened to birds and animals. The kinship of the God of the prophets is with human persons.

2. Jer. 3. 19.
3. Deut. 32. 18.
4. Isa. 36. 3 (Joah = Yah(weh) is brother).
5. Hos. 2. 16.
6. Jer. 3. 4.
7. Isa. 63. 1, 2.
8. Ezek. 34. 31.
9. Amos 9. 9.
10. Ezek. 22. 20.
11. Amos 7. 7.
12. Isa. 45. 9.
13. Isa. 4. 4; cf. Jer. 2. 22.
14. Deut. 32. 39.
15. Isa. 33. 22.
16. Isa. 55. 1, 2.
17. Jer. 10. 10.
18. Jer. 31. 33.

When the Hebrews claimed that their God was the *living God*,[19] they meant what they said and demonstrated in their theological method the courage of their convictions. They displayed no reticence, for example, in ascribing to him the most human of emotions, like repentance, indignation, impatience, pain, exultation, sorrow, compassion, joy, anger, vengeance, scorn, hatred and love. Such a list could be extended almost indefinitely, but it will serve its purpose if it suggests that we fall into ludicrous error when we select one or two of these metaphors and then proceed to interpret them as precise and formal theological terms.

It is obvious enough that some of this language suggests a conception of God that falls short of the best we know in ordinary human experience, but we must be very clear about what features of it we ought to reject. Too often, theologians have dismissed nearly the whole of it as 'childish anthropomorphism' or '*mere* metaphor', as if to suggest that the adult mind can dispense with the use of analogy. Such sophistication is pitiful self-deception. Metaphor – *mere* metaphor – is all we have to help us communicate (both to ourselves and others) our understanding of God, no matter how discreetly we try to disguise the fact by organizing a selection of images into a system of doctrinal propositions. Such figures as the 'fatherhood' of God, the 'kingship' of God, the 'wrath' of God, the 'love' of God, and all the rest remain metaphorical, because they were and still are at some point anchored in human experience. They would be incomprehensible (and, therefore, useless) if they were not. If only we could stop dehydrating the poetry of the prophets and discover once again that it provides a 'sacramental' approach to the common ways of God and humanity, our account of their faith would be purged of some of the shrivelled and lifeless language with which it is encumbered.

The prophets demonstrated their sovereign independence not only by ransacking everyday experience for living words with which to communicate the Word of the living God, but

19. Jer. 10. 10; 23. 36; Ps. 18. 46; 42. 2; II Sam. 12. 5; 14. 11; 15. 21.

also by exploiting in their preaching all kinds of conventional forms of speech, both sacred and secular.

Thus, for example, Isaiah adopts a form of legal indictment current in the courts to give ironic force to his exposure of those who were supposed to be responsible for the administration of justice:

> The LORD comes forward to argue his case
> and stands to judge his people.
> The LORD opens the indictment
> against the elders of his people and their officers:
> You have ravaged the vineyard,
> and the spoils of the poor are in your houses.
> Is it nothing to you that you crush my people
> and grind the faces of the poor?
> This is the very word of the Lord, the LORD of Hosts.[20]

Another legal form often taken over by the prophets for their oracles of judgement is the 'law-suit' speech, of the kind which was used after the breach of an international treaty, with its identifiable elements of introduction, interrogation, charge, verdict and sentence.[21]

No professional preserve was spared the prophets' daring imitations, as when Hosea adapts the regular liturgical form for a lament,[22] Amos a funeral dirge[23] and Isaiah (with calculated insolence) the form of oral instruction given by a priest to a layman:

> Hear the word of the LORD, you rulers of Sodom;
> attend, you people of Gomorrah, to the instruction of our God:
> Your countless sacrifices, what are they to me?
> says the LORD.

20. Isa. 3. 13–15 (NEB).
21. Jer. 2. 4–13; 6. 18–21; Mic. 6. 1–8; Isa. 42. 18–25; 48. 12–16; 57. 3–13; 58. 1–14; cf. I Kgs. 14. 7–11; 21. 17–24.
22. Hos. 6. 1–3; cf. Ezek. 19. 1–14.
23. Amos 5. 2; cf. Isa. 14. 4–21.

I am sated with whole-offerings of rams
   and the fat of buffaloes;
I have no desire for the blood of bulls,
   of sheep and of he-goats.
Whenever you come to enter my presence –
   who asked you for this?
No more shall you trample my courts.
The offer of your gifts is useless,
   the reek of sacrifice is abhorrent to me.
New moons and sabbaths and assemblies,
   sacred seasons and ceremonies, I cannot endure.
I cannot tolerate your new moons and your festivals;
   they have become a burden to me,
   and I can put up with them no longer.
When you lift your hands outspread in prayer,
I will hide my eyes from you.
Though you offer countless prayers,
   I will not listen.
There is blood on your hands;
   wash yourselves and be clean.
Put away the evil of your deeds,
   away out of my sight.
Cease to do evil and learn to do right,
   pursue justice and champion the oppressed;
   give the orphan his rights, plead the widow's cause.[24]

Instruction was given in Israel not only by priests but by teachers who educated the country's civil servants and the prophets' preaching abounds in snatches taken from the classroom – parables,[25] sharp rhetorical questions with their appeal to common sense,[26] consecutive numbers in pairs,[27] and proverbial sayings.[28] It is to Israel's school teachers that

24. Isa. 1. 10–17 (NEB); cf. Isa. 8. 11–15; Hag. 2. 12–14.
25. Isa. 28. 23–9; cf. II Sam. 12. 1–6.
26. Amos 3. 3–8; Isa. 10. 15; 29. 15, 16; Jer. 8. 4, 5; 13. 22, 23; 18. 13–15; cf. Prov. 6. 27, 28; 30. 4; Job 8. 11.
27. Amos 1. 3–2. 8; cf. Prov. 6. 16–19; 30. 15–11.
28. Hos. 4. 11 (cf. Prov. 20. 1); 4. 14 (cf. Prov. 10. 8, 10).

we must also ascribe the prophets' fondness for drawing attention to the lessons to be learnt from nature, as Job did later:

> But ask the beasts, and they will teach you;
> ask the birds of the air to inform you,
> or tell the creatures that crawl to teach you,
> and the fish of the sea to instruct you.[29]

Both Isaiah and Jeremiah contrast the knowledge of the beasts and birds with Israel's lamentable lack of it:

> Sons have I reared and brought up,
>   but they have rebelled against me.
> The ox knows its owner,
>   and the ass its master's crib;
> but Israel does not know,
>   my people does not understand.
>
> Even the stork in the heavens
>   knows her times;
> And the turtledove, swallow, and crane
>   keep the time of their coming;
> but my people know not
>   the ordinance of the LORD.[30]

It is hardly fortuitous that Isaiah's rebuke is remarkably similar to that administered in a standard school text from ancient Egypt, which points to the teachability of the cow and the horse, in order to put to shame the unteachable pupil:

> And the cow will be fetched this year and will plough on the return of the year: it begins to hearken to the herdsman; it can all but speak. Horses brought from the field have forgotten their dams; they are yoked and go up and down on every manner of errand for His Majesty. They become like those

29. Job 12. 7, 8 (REB).
30. Isa. 1. 2, 3; Jer. 8. 7; cf. Jer. 5. 20–9.

that bore them, and they stand in the stable, whilst they do absolutely everything for fear of a beating. *Even if I beat you with any kind of stick, you do not hearken.*[31]

The immense variety and sheer impertinence of the prophets' forms of speech afford significant evidence of the range of their concern and their fearlessness in pursuing it. They spoke everyday language, because nothing was beyond the province of the God from whom they had received their commission. As laymen, they were free from all the inhibitions of professional groups and sectional interests and, as *educated* laymen, they were equipped to play an unprecedented role in making articulate the radical implications of Israel's traditional faith.

THE RIGHTEOUSNESS OF THE PROPHETS

'The LORD sent Nathan the prophet to David.' With these words, the curtain rises on one of the most exquisite and effective narratives in the Old Testament.[32] David is told a parable by the prophet about how a poor man had been callously deprived of his solitary ewe lamb:

There were two men in a certain city, the one rich and the other poor. The rich man had very many flocks and herds; but the poor man had nothing but one little ewe lamb, which he had bought. And he brought it up, and it grew up with him and with his children; it used to eat of his morsel, and drink from his cup, and lie in his bosom, and it was like a daughter to him. Now there came a traveller to the rich man, and he was unwilling to take one of his own flock or herd to prepare for the wayfarer who had come to him, but he took the poor man's lamb, and prepared it for the man who had come to him.[33]

31. See R. A. Caminos, *Late-Egyptian Miscellanies*, p. 377.
32. II Sam. 12. 1–15.
33. II Sam. 12. 1–4.

David fell into Nathan's trap and, in roundly condemning the rich man 'because he had no pity,' unwittingly passed judgement on his own theft of Bathsheba from Uriah, her lawful husband. Little did the king expect the devastating climax: 'Nathan said to David, "You are the man." '

This story gives us the flavour of the prophets' moral sensitivity and a hint of their extraordinary courage. Also from the early prophetic tradition comes the comparable story of how Elijah championed the cause of one of Ahab's subjects, when the king's notorious wife, Jezebel, murdered him to get possession of his vineyard. The narrative makes it clear that much more than a theory about private property or a dispute about compensation was involved:

> Now Naboth the Jezreelite had a vineyard in Jezreel, beside the palace of Ahab king of Samaria. And after this Ahab said to Naboth, 'Give me your vineyard, that I may have it for a vegetable garden, because it is near my house; and I will give you a better vineyard for it; or, if it seems good to you, I will give you its value in money.' But Naboth said to Ahab, 'The LORD forbid that I should give you the inheritance of my fathers.' And Ahab went into his house vexed and sullen because of what Naboth the Jezreelite had said to him; for he had said, 'I will not give you the inheritance of my fathers.' And he lay down on his bed, and turned away his face, and would eat no food.[34]

The man who wrote this account clearly had a deep loathing for the type of tyrant who thinks that he can buy out a man's self-respect. In Israel, a man's family property was reckoned an integral part of himself,[35] and the narrator was concerned to show how the prophet upheld (as we should say) 'what it means to be a person' against interference even from the head of the state. The large-scale confiscation of property in the eighth and seventh centuries BC shows how the tradition of

34. I Kgs. 21. 1–4.
35. Jer. 32. 6–12; Lev. 25. 25–34; Ezek. 46. 16–18.

equality and brotherhood, enjoined by the Mosaic faith, had been eroded by the new 'civilized' standards of the kingdom.[36] The prophets strenuously denounced all such grabbing, because it manifested a fundamental indifference to the dignity of human beings. Hear Micah on the subject:

> Woe to those who devise wickedness
>   and work evil upon their beds!
> When the morning dawns, they perform it,
>   because it is in the power of their hand.
> They covet fields, and seize them;
>   and houses, and take them away;
> they oppress a man and his house,
>   a man and his inheritance.[37]

Because it is in the power of their hand. Again, Micah's condemnation of this aggressive society is more than an economic judgement. His sense of outrage springs from an appreciation of the rights and responsibilities of men and women before God. The righteousness of the prophet is the righteousness of God himself.

It is abundantly clear that the People of God had accepted the debased standards of a competitive society and had lost the personal integrity their ancestors had learnt in the days of Moses. Small and eccentric groups – like the Rechabites and Nazirites – still clung conservatively to parts of the ancient tradition, but they were too withdrawn from ordinary society to exercise any general influence.[38] Much as the prophets upheld the standards of early Israel,[39] their cry was not simply 'Return to the desert', but 'Return to the God of the Exodus.' They alone effectively revolted against the corruption and cruelty that cried to high heaven on every side.

The eighth century BC in its earlier phase had been

36. I Sam. 8. 14, 15; Jer. 22. 13–19; Deut. 17. 14–17.
37. Mic. 2. 1, 2; cf. 2. 8, 9; Isa. 2. 7; 3. 14; 5. 8; Amos 4. 1; Exod. 20. 17.
38. Jer. 35. 1–19; II Kgs. 10. 15–28; Num. 6. 1–21; Amos 2. 11, 12.
39. Jer. 2. 2, 3; Hos. 2. 15; 9. 10; 11. 1, 2.

enjoying a post-war boom almost without precedent. Damascus in the north and Assyria to the far north-east were
too busily preoccupied with their own concerns to interfere
in Israel's national life. The period from about 785 to 745
BC was therefore a veritable gala-time for the ambitious and
the unprincipled *nouveaux riches*. The reaction of Amos is
characteristic:

> Woe to those who are at ease in Zion,
> and to those who feel secure on the
>   mountain of Samaria,
> the notable men of the first of the nations,
> to whom the house of Israel come!
> Woe to those who lie upon beds of ivory,
> and stretch themselves upon their couches,
> and eat lambs from the flock,
> and calves from the midst of the stall;
> who sing idle songs to the sound of the harp,
> and like David invent for themselves
>   instruments of music;
> who drink wine in bowls,
> and anoint themselves with the finest oils,
> but are not grieved over the ruin of Joseph!
> Therefore they shall now be the first of those
>   to go into exile,
> and the revelry of those who stretch themselves shall
>   pass away.[40]

These idle sprawlers, luxuriating in their choice lamb and
especially fattened veal ('from the midst of the stall'), lolling
about with their lutes, soaking themselves in drink (taking it
not by the cup but by the bowl), and regaling themselves with
the finest cosmetics, are pilloried here with unsurpassed invective. They will be the first, says Amos, to suffer in the
coming judgement of the nation, which their feckless indifference has hastened.

40. Amos 6. 1, 4–7; cf. 2. 6, 7; 4. 1–3; 5. 10–13; Isa. 1. 23; 3. 16–4. 1; 5. 8–13.

The prophets were violent, because they lived in a society where honesty and decency were being violated every day. They could not profess a vocation from the Lord, the God of righteousness, and stand aloof when disgusting luxury was being purchased at the price of the blood of the defenceless poor:

> For wicked men are found among my people;
>> they lurk like fowlers lying in wait.
> They set a trap;
>> they catch men.
> Like a basket full of birds,
>> their houses are full of treachery;
> therefore they have become great and rich,
>> they have grown fat and sleek.
> They know no bounds in deeds of wickedness;
>> they judge not with justice
> the cause of the fatherless, to make it prosper,
>> and they do not defend the rights
>> of the needy.
> Shall I not punish them for these things?
>> says the LORD,
>> and shall I not avenge myself
>> on a nation such as this?[41]

It was only too easy in the age of the prophets to swindle the helpless,[42] to exploit human want by usury,[43] to get away with sharp practice in business dealings (underweighing and over-charging),[44] to murder and rob,[45] and then to evade punishment by bribing the judges.[46] A person's word was too light a thing to stand in the way of ambition and greed.[47]

41. Jer. 5. 26–9.
42. Amos 5. 11; Mic. 3. 1–3; Ezek. 22. 29; Mal. 3. 5; Isa. 10. 1, 2.
43. Ezek. 18. 10–13; 22. 12; Hab. 2. 6, 7; Exod. 22. 25–7; Deut. 23. 19, 20.
44. Amos 8. 4–6; Deut. 25. 13–16.
45. Hos. 4. 1–3; 6. 8, 9; 7. 1; Isa. 1. 21; Jer. 7. 9, 10; Ezek. 7. 23; 9. 9; 11. 6.
46. Amos 5. 12; 6. 12; Mic. 3. 9–11; Isa. 5. 22, 23; 10. 1, 2; Zeph. 3. 3.
47. Hos. 4. 1, 2; Jer. 34. 8–17.

The fearlessness with which the prophets let their conscience speak against this travesty of human conduct reveals the quality of their moral awareness. It had been informed and empowered in a manner quite without precedent by their personal knowledge of God. For them, inhuman cruelty was nothing less than religious apostasy, because it disrupted the family life of God's people and denied the sovereignty of the Righteous One.

RELIGION AND RIGHTEOUSNESS

What the prophets found in society was not only cruelty, but cruelty masquerading under the cloak of piety. Jeremiah, perhaps more than any other member of the goodly fellowship, was literally appalled by such hypocrisy:

> Will you steal, murder, commit adultery, swear falsely, burn incense to Baal, and go after other gods that you have not known, and then come and stand before me in this house, which is called by my name, and say, 'We are delivered!' – only to go on doing all these abominations? Has this house, which is called by my name, become a den of robbers in your eyes? Behold, I myself have seen it, says the LORD.[48]

With comparable horror, Amos exposed the licentious behaviour that passed for religious observance at Israel's local sanctuaries:

> A man and his father go in to the
> same maiden,
> so that my holy name is profaned;
> they lay themselves down beside every altar
> upon garments taken in pledge;
> and in the house of their God they drink
> the wine of those who have been fined.[49]

48. Jer. 7. 9–11.
49. Amos 2. 7, 8; cf. Hos. 4. 14; Deut. 23. 17; Exod. 22. 26, 27; Prov. 15. 8; 21. 3, 27.

The stark discrepancy between people's rebellion against God by inhumanity to their fellows and their enthusiastic performance of religious rites completely revolted the prophets. It clearly showed that such worship was in no sense whatsoever an outward and visible sign of an inward and spiritual communion: 'Thou art near in their mouth and far from their heart.'[50] Although it must in fairness be said that we have no reason to suppose that everybody who practised sacrifice was a contemptible formalist, or that the life of all Israelite sanctuaries was devoid of spiritual significance, the evidence suggests that in the eighth and seventh centuries BC the cult was very deeply paganized. Israel's trouble was not a lack of religion, but an excess of it. It is not surprising, therefore, that whenever the great prophets speak of the sacrificial worship of the sanctuaries, their words burn with indignation and loathing: 'For God's sake, stop it!' That was their message.[51]

Curious students of the prophetic writings have not been content to leave the matter there. Granted, they say, that the prophets condemned the abuse of sacrifice, did they also condemn sacrifice *in itself* and wish to abolish it entirely? The ensuing debate has generated more heat than light. It seems that the argument will never be concluded, for the simple reason that the distinction between sacrifice as practised and sacrifice in itself is not a distinction that would have occurred to the prophets themselves. When we press the theoretical question, therefore, all our evidence is indirect and ambiguous. What is quite unambiguous is the fact that the cult they saw before their very eyes they wholeheartedly detested.

Those who maintain that the prophets could not have intended any more than the reform of the debased worship of the sanctuaries, because it is impossible to conceive how Israel's worship could have continued without sacrifice in one

50. Jer. 12. 2; cf. Isa. 29. 13; Mark 7. 6, 7.
51. Amos 4. 4, 5; 5. 21–5; Hos. 5. 6; 6. 6; 8. 11–13; Isa. 1. 10–17; Mic. 6. 6–8; Jer. 6. 19–21; 7. 21–8; 11. 15; Isa. 66. 1–4; I Sam. 15. 22; cf. Isa. 43. 22–4; 58. 3–9.

form or another, must find more compelling reasons for their confidence. Both Amos and Jeremiah flatly claimed (whether rightly or wrongly is wholly irrelevant) that sacrifice was no part of Israel's worship in the days of Moses;[52] after the fall of Jerusalem, the Jews of the Dispersion worshipped without sacrifice; and the Christian Church repudiated it.[53] It is hardly possible to maintain, therefore, that animal sacrifice was an essential part even of Jewish religious practice. Nor is it possible to attach much importance to the prophets' failure to propose an alternative to the normal cult, since none of them was an ecclesiastical planner and many of them, in any case, believed that the people had little future to plan for.

Those who take the view that the prophets simply wanted to rid the cult of its abuses sometimes lean on the fact that their oracles were preserved by a post-exilic tradition which not only accepted sacrifice, but found in it genuine joy and delight. This line of argument assumes that the editors of the Hebrew scriptures never allowed anything of which they themselves did not thoroughly approve to slip through their fingers. This assumption cannot survive a moment's scrutiny of the evidence. Nobody who pauses to consider the conflicting regulations of the law books, the astonishing juxtapositions in the Psalter, the contradictory narratives that have been allowed to stand in the historical books, not to mention the glaringly obvious reinterpretations in the books of the prophets, will be able to subscribe to the theory that the transmitters and editors of the Old Testament rigorously deleted material which presented an outlook at variance with their own. They left their mark not by deletion but by addition.[54] It is therefore very far from certain that the prophets must have shared the views of the men who collected and preserved their oracles.

What is certain and very revealing is the prophets' spontaneous and vigorous repudiation of the practice current in

52. Amos 5. 25; Jer. 7. 22.
53. Heb. 10. 4–9; Mark 12. 28–34; Matt. 9. 10–13; 12. 1–8.
54. See pp. 7–8, 13–18, 23.

their day. It is not only what they said that carries weight, but the utterly scornful indignation with which they said it; as, for example, when Jeremiah lumps together the whole-offerings, which were not eaten by the worshippers, with those that were and tells the people (since God is not interested) to eat the whole lot themselves: 'Add your whole-offerings to your sacrifices and eat the flesh your-selves.'[55] Even more significant, however, is the fact that when the prophets attack the cult, they explicitly contrast it with their own unambiguous understanding of what is really meant by devotion and obedience to God:

I hate, I despise your feasts,
and I take no delight in your
    solemn assemblies.
Even though you offer me your
burnt offerings and cereal offerings,
I will not accept them,
and the peace offerings of your fatted
    beasts
I will not look upon.
Take away from me the noise of
    your songs;
to the melody of your harps I will
    not listen.
But let justice roll down like waters,
and righteousness like an
    ever-flowing stream.[56]

The service which God demands is *righteousness of life*. If we believe that the prophets' emphasis was mistaken, it is better to admit it without prevarication than to smudge their con-victions in order that we may continue to walk in their company. That at least some later Israelite circles accepted

55. Jer. 7. 21 (REB); compare the irony of Amos 4. 4, 5.
56. Amos 5. 21–4; compare the same contrast in most of the passages listed on p. 69.

and developed this interpretation of the prophets' teaching is evident from more than one passage of the Psalter:

> Hear, O my people, and I will speak,
>   O Israel, I will testify against you.
>   I am God, your God.
> I do not reprove you for your sacrifices;
>   your burnt offerings are continually before me.
> I will accept no bull from your house,
>   nor he-goat from your folds.
> For every beast of the forest is mine,
>   the cattle on a thousand hills.
> I know all the birds of the air,
>   and all that moves in the field is mine.
>
> If I were hungry, I would not tell you;
>   for the world and all that is in it is mine.
> Do I eat the flesh of bulls,
>   or drink the blood of goats?
> Offer to God a sacrifice of thanksgiving,
>   and pay your vows to the Most High;
> and call upon me in the day of trouble;
>   I will deliver you, and you shall glorify me.[57]

This calm exposure of the futility of animal holocausts is a persuasive confirmation of the prophets' unrestrained invective.

THE RIGHTEOUSNESS OF GOD

When the message of the Hebrew prophets began to stimulate new interest in the last century, it was almost inevitable that it should have been interpreted primarily as a call for social righteousness. Such was the temper of the times. As we have seen, the prophets strongly emphasized this demand of true religion and what they said in the eighth and seventh centuries BC is still very much to the point. It is necessary to insist,

57. Ps. 50. 7–15; cf. Ps. 40. 6–8; 51. 15–17; Isa. 40. 16; 58. 3–9.

however, that the prophets' 'social gospel' was rooted and grounded in God. Their moral insight and power are inexplicable apart from their religion.

As soon as we begin to use the word 'religion' in speaking of the prophets, the suspicion arises that it is not, perhaps, the best way of describing their characteristic faith. We need a term which makes it clear that 'religion', as they conceived it, was not a special kind of activity, for which some few people are equipped by their having been endowed with a particular kind of temperament. What the prophets were concerned with was the moral and spiritual life of the whole community – the community God himself had called into being, and in which he could be *known* by the care and affection of its members for each other. Thus, for example, Jeremiah said of Josiah:

> He judged the cause of the poor and needy;
> then it was well.
> Is not this to *know* me?
> says the LORD.[58]

Righteousness was not a duty imposed by religion; it *was* religion, the way, that is to say, of knowing and serving God. The best method of exploring this prophetic understanding is to investigate what they meant by the righteousness of God.

Basically, the term 'righteous' (*çédheq*) in the Old Testament means that which is regarded as being standard and normal. Thus, for example, it was used to describe 'just' or standard weights and measures.[59] To be 'righteous' means, therefore, to conform to the accepted standard, to be 'in the right'. Fundamentally, the term is a legal and not a moral one, as is obvious from the fact that you are 'put in the right' (but not, of course, made *morally* righteous) when a wrong is committed against you.[60] In disputed cases, it is

58. Jer. 22. 16.
59. Ezek. 45. 10; Deut. 25. 15; Lev. 19. 36.
60. Ezek. 16. 51, 52; Gen. 38. 26; I Sam. 24. 17.

the business of a judge to decide who is 'in the right'. By dispensing justice, he maintains the *norm* of society; in giving judgement, he declares one party 'guilty' and the other party 'innocent' – by reference, always, to the *normal* standard (the law). It is clear that justice ('rightness') and the judgements by which it is expressed and maintained are closely related, and more obviously so in a society where much of the law is uncodified custom. It is not surprising, therefore, that the Hebrew term for the judgement or legal decision (*mishpāṭ*) pronounced by a judge (*shôphēṭ*) is also used in the Old Testament to mean the 'done thing', the customary manner of life in a community, or (more generally) what has been accepted as right and fitting.[61]

A particular manner of life was right and fitting for Israel, the people with whom God had entered into an intimate covenant relationship. The norm of this new community was not merely traditional social custom, but the character and will of God to whom it owed its creation and preservation. The righteousness which the prophets demand is invariably the righteousness of God.[62] The contrast between the righteousness God expected of his people and the rebellion he suffered from them is forcefully stated in the climax of Isaiah's 'Song of the Vineyard':

> For the vineyard of the LORD of hosts
> is the house of Israel,
> and the men of Judah
> are his pleasant planting;
> and he looked for justice [*mishpāṭ*],
> but behold, bloodshed [*mispāḥ*]
> for righteousness [*çedhāqāh*],
> but behold, a cry [*çeʿāqāh*].[63]

---

61. I Kgs. 18. 28; II Kgs. 17. 33; Judg. 13. 12; 18. 7; I Sam. 27. 11; Exod. 26. 30; I Kgs. 6. 38.
62. Jer. 9. 23, 24; Hos. 2. 19; 10. 12; Isa. 28. 17; Zeph. 3. 5.
63. Isa. 5. 7.

This powerful play on words can hardly be represented in English. God expected morality and found murder, riotousness instead of righteousness.

When, in the prophetic books, we read that 'the LORD has a controversy with his people,'[64] legal language is again being used. The image is that of a court of law before which Israel stands accused; sometimes God is the prosecutor, more often he is the judge. The judgements he delivers not only condemn evil-doers[65] but also (and at the same time) vindicate the oppressed, which is in line with the fact that to 'judge' the oppressed in the Old Testament always means to deliver them.[66]

God, however, was more than the Judge of Israel; he was Judge of the whole world.[67] This prophetic conviction is clear in the first two chapters of Amos, which make a tremendous sweep through the nations on Israel's borders, pronouncing doom on each for its notorious conduct and finally coming home with accumulated momentum to condemn Israel itself.[68] Similarly, Isaiah, who shared Amos' conviction that his own people were on trial in the divine court, also affirms that God's judgement is not limited to Israel; it will be pronounced on the arrogant boasting of the king of Assyria.[69] Second Isaiah, therefore, had good precedent in the prophetic tradition for representing Israel's God as Judge of all the earth. In his time, the case to be decided was no longer one between the innocent and the guilty within Israel, but one between Israel and its external oppressors. In a series of trial scenes,[70] the nations are summoned to appear before the divine Judge:

Assemble yourselves and come,
   draw near together,
   you survivors of the nations!

64. Mic. 6. 2; cf. Hos. 4. 1; Isa. 1. 2–4; 3. 13; Jer. 2. 9.
65. Ezek. 7. 3; 11. 10.
66. Isa. 1. 17, 23; Jer. 22. 16; Ps. 72. 4.
67. Gen. 18. 25.
68. Amos 1. 3–2. 16; see pp. 144–5.
69. Isa. 10. 12–16; 14. 24–7; 37. 22–9.
70. Isa. 41. 1–5, 21–9; 43. 8–15; 44. 6–8; 45. 20–5.

They have no knowledge
  who carry about their wooden idols,
and keep on praying to a god
  that cannot save.
Declare and present your case;
  let them take counsel together!
Who told this long ago?
  Who declared it of old?
Was it not I, the LORD?
  And there is no other god besides me,
a righteous God and a Saviour;
  there is none besides me.[71]

The essential point to grasp is that, for the prophets, the righteousness of God found expression both in judgement *on* wickedness and in salvation *from* wickedness. So Second Isaiah declares that God is a 'righteous God and a Saviour'. He is both at the same time and for the same reason. His righteousness is manifested in the acts by which he brought Israel into being, when he called the people out of Egypt,[72] the acts by which he condemns wicked offenders against his moral order, and the acts by which he delivers his people from the nations who seek to destroy it.[73] No other term so fully expresses the character and purpose of God and the ultimate significance for the world of Israel's life and history.

The word 'righteousness', of course, provides only a framework of reference and in itself tells us nothing about the content of God's revealed character and purpose. That we must discover by observing its specific manifestations in the story of Israel. It is, however, most illuminating to find that the prophets are able to use this one term to describe (*a*) the purposeful activity of God in history; (*b*) the moral 'law' of the universe; and (*c*) the source and goal of Israel's unique

71. Isa. 45. 20, 21.
72. Exod. 6. 6; 7. 4; cf. Mic. 6. 5; Ps. 103. 6, 7; Judg. 5. 11; I Sam. 12. 7.
73. Isa. 41. 10; 45. 8; 46. 13; 51. 5; 62. 11; cf. Isa. 11. 4, 5; Jer. 23. 6; Hos. 2. 19; Mic. 7. 9.

vocation. It means, in other words, that they were quite unaware of our distinction between religion and ethics, response to God and response to our fellow men and women. In the terms of prophetic faith, you simply cannot be moral without serving and revealing God; you cannot be 'godly' without serving your neighbour; and you cannot serve the community without being both moral *and* 'godly'.

We can trace the same fundamental interrelationship in the prophets' conception of the opposite of righteousness – sin. Outside the prophetic tradition, sin was primarily an offence against God's holiness and many so-called sins were little more than ritual breaches of a taboo. Like the 'unwitting' sins described in the post-exilic law books (but, perhaps, derived from ancient tradition), they are devoid of anything we easily recognize as morally significant.[74] The prophets, however, radically departed from this whole outlook. They declared that what principally constituted sin against God was people's cruelty to one another. When a man treated his neighbour callously, he was offending against the righteousness of God. Inhumanity was a *religious* offence. We entirely miss the impact of the first section of the book of Amos, in which the prophet castigates the nations for their crimes against each other by the standards of common humanity (and not, as we might expect, for their crimes against Israel), unless we appreciate that such conduct is declared to be *an act of rebellion against the God of Israel*:

> Thus says the LORD:
> 'For three transgressions of the Ammonites,
>   and for four, I will not revoke the
>   punishment;
>   because they have ripped up women with child
>   in Gilead,
>   that they might enlarge their border.'

74. I Sam. 14. 24–45; II Sam. 6. 6, 7; 24. 1–25; Lev. 4; 5. 1–4; 22. 14.

Thus says the LORD:
'For three transgressions of Moab,
   and for four, I will not revoke the
      punishment;
   because he burned to lime
      the bones of the king of Edom.'[75]

There is no question here of breaking a code of law, as the translation 'transgression' may suggest. The Hebrew word *pésha'* means rebellion against a person.[76] What the prophet said, therefore, was 'for three acts of *rebellion* [against God], God will not turn back the devastating doom'. Cruelty, wherever it was to be found, was a defiant spurning of the distinctively human privilege of 'walking with God'.[77]

Apart from using expressions of a quasi-technical character, the prophets plundered their experience and their vocabulary to bring home to Israel the meaning of its wickedness. In the language of the householder, it was filthy and needed God's cleansing,[78] in the language of the surgeon, it was desperately wounded and needed God's healing hand;[79] in the language of the shepherd, it was a lost sheep, whom God must lead back to the fold;[80] in the language of the farmer, it was grain choked with rubbish;[81] in the language of the metal-worker, it was full of dross and needed God to smelt it;[82] in the language of the builder, it invited demolition;[83] in the language of the slave market, it had sold itself and awaited redemption by its next of kin.[84]

These homely terms leave us in no doubt that the intimate relationship between God and Israel was not regarded by the

75. Amos 1. 13; 2. 1.
76. II Kgs. 3. 5; I Kgs. 12. 19.
77. Gen. 5. 22, 24; 6. 9; Mic. 6. 8; Mal. 2. 6.
78. Jer. 2. 22.
79. Isa. 1. 5, 6.
80. Jer. 23. 3.
81. Amos 9. 9.
82. Ezek. 22. 18–22.
83. Amos 7. 8.
84. Isa. 50. 1.

prophets as an intimacy between equals. It was the privileged relationship of an erring son to a father, whose authority in the ancient world (it is easy to forget) was beyond dispute.[85] The norm, that is to say, the 'righteousness', of Israel's family life was the absolute righteousness of its head, and for this, human experience provided no more than a hint. We noticed earlier how the prophets were conscious of the inadequacy of all human language for describing the God whom they were called to obey and yet how characteristically and superbly his sovereignty is disclosed in their vivid and concrete analogies. In their appeal to human experience and in their recognition of its limitations, they anticipate the teaching of Jesus:

> If you then, who are evil, know how to give good gifts to your children, how much more will your Father who is in heaven give good things to those who ask him![86]

The *how much more* of this saying is not only the ladder set between earth and heaven; it is also the measure of the difference between the Creator and his creatures.

85. Jer. 7. 23.
86. Matt. 7. 11.

CHAPTER 5

Judgement Without Promise

Salvation is the fundamental concept of all religions. Where they differ is in the content they give to salvation and in the conditions they require to be satisfied before it may be enjoyed. In the religion of Israel, salvation was the presupposition and goal of priest and prophet alike and between them they covered the whole range from salvation as physical welfare to salvation as fellowship with God in the new life of the Age to Come. The priests and prophets of Israel worked, however, not as private individuals, but as the agents and spokesmen for a received religious tradition and the diversity of their outlook is largely to be accounted for by the diversity of their inheritance.

Broadly speaking, Israel's religious life was shaped by two principal concepts of the relationship of the people with their God. The earlier and more profound concept traced not only the beginning of Israel's relationship with God, but the beginning and ground of its very existence as a people, to the Exodus from Egypt. This deliverance, it was believed, established a bond of mutual obligation between them, which was formally ratified in the Mosaic covenant.[1] Israel thus set out on a journey through history in company with its God, but what happened in the future depended, as must always be the case in a personal relationship, on their mutual fidelity. This conditional element is reflected (albeit imperfectly) in the Old Testament's understanding of obedience to the Law. The second concept, which was borrowed from the neighbouring imperial powers with the institution of the Hebrew monarchy, was based on a political rather than a personal model. It held that God, the Creator and King of the Universe,

1. Hos. 2. 14, 15; I Sam. 12. 7, 8.

had chosen Israel to act as his vicegerent in the world and, for this purpose, had delegated his sovereign power to the royal house of David.[2]

These two basic concepts of the 'covenant' relationship – personal and *therefore* conditional, political and *therefore* unconditional – are difficult to disentangle in the complexities of the Old Testament material. In the preaching of the independent prophets, however, the personal concept of the Mosaic tradition is expressed with unprecedented clarity and developed to its ultimate conclusion. The prophets' insistence on the conditional nature of God's relationship with his people inevitably brought them into conflict with the theology of the royal sanctuaries, which admitted no doubts about Israel's unconditional salvation.

AMOS

The essential point to grasp about the first of the 'classical' prophets, who preached in the northern kingdom in the middle of the eighth century BC, is that he was an educated and morally sensitive layman, who came to see absolutely everything in the light of the reality and activity of God. Amos ascribed this overwhelming awareness to a direct and dramatic summons by God himself and there is no better way of accounting for it. As a result, he exposed the religion and social conduct of Israel to a scrutiny of unprecedented rigour and came to the conclusion that it was impossible that they could be allowed to continue. What precisely Amos meant by God's destruction of Israel, we do not know. It is as difficult to suppose that he expected the literal physical annihilation of the whole people, as it is unwise to interpret his message merely as a demand for certain reforms expressed in urgent and somewhat exaggerated language. At the very least, Amos taught that Israel had withdrawn from its special relationship to God and, therefore, that its distinctive existence as the

2. II Sam. 7. 14–17; 23. 5; Ps. 21. 7; 68. 7–16; 78. 67–72; 89. 1–4, 19–37; Jer. 33. 19–22; see pp. 96–9, 137–8, 141–3.

people of God was coming to an end. The sovereign Lord of all the families of the earth had freely chosen Israel at the beginning of its history; its election was now cancelled. This cancellation was the very reverse of capricious. No prophet expounds more clearly than Amos the reason for God's judgement: *Israel was doomed because it was spiritually and morally dead.* All the oracles of Amos convey this single stark conviction.

Amos' shattering dismissal of his contemporaries' religious confidence exposed Israel's drift from its original austerely moral faith to a syncretistic cult which promised the people unconditional security. It is, therefore, fearless independence rather than conscious innovation which gives the work of Amos so high a degree of importance, although only a man of great originality could, in the confused religious situation of his day, have recaptured so clearly and developed so radically the basic character of Israel's traditional faith. That is why his radicalism not only reaffirmed the old Mosaic faith, but inaugurated a new phase in his people's religious awareness.

Amos cultivated the practice of embodying in his oracles quotations of his opponents' claims (before proceeding to cast them in their teeth) and this provides an illuminating confirmation of the confidence which had been engendered by the religion of the sanctuaries. From his contemporaries' unqualified conviction that 'The Lord of hosts is with us'[3] sprang the smug assurance that 'Evil shall not overtake or meet us.'[4] Such was their 'fancied security',[5] that they looked forward to the time when God would make good the triumphal assertion that was presented in their religious festivals and act decisively to vanquish their enemies and finally establish Israel as 'the first of the nations'.[6] They called this day of vindication the Day of the Lord and Amos' reversal of its popular meaning sums up the whole of his message:

3. Amos 5. 14; cf. 6. 1–3.
4. Amos 9. 10.
5. Zeph. 2. 15.
6. Amos 6. 1.

Woe to you who desire the day of the LORD!
  Why would you have the day of the LORD?
It is darkness, and not light . . .
Is not the day of the LORD darkness, and not light,
  and gloom with no brightness in it?[7]

Exactly how this expectation established itself in popular piety is still a matter of debate. The most clearly marked features that constantly recur in the later (and more conventional) prophetic oracles on the Day of the Lord appear to have their origin in the ancient Near Eastern concept of Holy War. First, in these oracles, God musters his troops:

Hark, a tumult on the mountains as of a great multitude!
Hark, an uproar of kingdoms, of nations gathering together!
The LORD of hosts is mustering a host for battle . . .
Wail, for the day of the LORD is near;
  as destruction from the Almighty it will come![8]

Even before the battle begins, the enemy is seized with panic:

Therefore all hands will be feeble,
  and every man's heart will melt,
  and they will be dismayed.
Pangs and agony will seize them;
  they will be in anguish like a woman in travail.
They will look aghast at one another;
  their faces will be aflame.[9]

During the battle, terrifying eruptions occur on the earth and in the heavens:

For the stars of the heavens and
  their constellations

7. Amos 5. 18–20.
8. Isa. 13. 4, 6; cf. Joel 2. 1.
9. Isa. 13. 7, 8; cf. Exod. 15. 14–16; Joel 2. 6.

> will not give their light;
> the sun will be dark at its rising
> and the moon will not shed its
>   light . . .
> Therefore I will make the heavens
>   tremble,
> and the earth will be shaken out
>   of its place,
> at the wrath of the LORD of hosts
>   in the day of his fierce anger.[10]

The battle ends with the complete destruction of the enemy:

> Behold, the day of the LORD comes,
>   cruel, with wrath and fierce anger,
> to make the earth a desolation
>   and to destroy its sinners from it.[11]

The most probable explanation of the survival of this 'Divine Warrior' language, long after Israel had ceased to think of its battles as engagement in Holy War, is that it had become established in the worship of the great sanctuaries during the period of the monarchy.[12] Here, we may suppose, it was associated with the claim that the Davidic kings, as 'the Lord's anointed', were agents of God's sovereignty over the nations. Psalm 18, for example, in which a Davidic king gives thanks to God for granting him victory in battle, uses the earth-shaking imagery of the thunderstorm to describe God's manifestation as a 'man of war':

> In my distress I called upon the LORD;
>   to my God I cried for help.
> From his temple he heard my voice,
>   and my cry to him reached his ears.

10. Isa. 13. 10, 13; cf. I Sam. 14. 15; Joel 2. 10.
11. Isa. 13. 9; cf. I Sam. 15. 2, 3; Joel 2. 20.
12. Cf. Ps. 46; 76; see pp. 144–5.

Then the earth reeled and rocked;
    the foundations also of the mountains trembled
    and quaked, because he was angry.
Smoke went up from his nostrils,
    and devouring fire from his mouth;
    glowing coals flamed forth from him.
He bowed the heavens, and came down;
    thick darkness was under his feet.
He rode on a cherub, and flew;
    he came swiftly upon the wings
    of the wind.
He made darkness his covering around him,
    his canopy thick clouds dark with water.
Out of the brightness before him
    there broke through his clouds
    hailstones and coals of fire.
The LORD also thundered in the heavens,
    and the Most High uttered his voice,
    hailstones and coals of fire.
And he sent out his arrows, and
    scattered them;
    he flashed forth lightnings, and
    routed them.
Then the channels of the sea were seen,
    and the foundations of the world
    were laid bare,
    at thy rebuke, O LORD,
    at the blast of the breath of thy nostrils . . .
Thou hast given me the shield of thy salvation,
    and thy right hand supported me,
    and thy help made me great . . .
I pursued my enemies and overtook them;
    and did not turn back till they were consumed.[13]

13. Ps. 18. 6–15, 35, 37; Exod. 15. 31; cf. Ps 2. 1–5, 8–12; 21. 8–12; 47. 2, 3; 89. 19–27; 110. 1, 2. The association of the motifs of Holy War with the claims of the Davidic kings, such as is found in Ps. 18, may well be indebted to the Egyptian tradition. For example, the Battle of Qadesh against the Hittites is presented as a Holy War, in which Ramesses II is the agent of Amun, his god:

Although much still remains obscure, we may safely conclude that the Day of the Lord to which Amos' contemporaries looked forward was part of the the liturgy of the sanctuaries and celebrated God's unconditional promise to save the king and his people by destroying their foreign foes. Amos boldly seizes the concept and redirects the destruction it proclaimed against Israel itself. What had symbolized the assurance of God's certain protection now became a declaration of Israel's certain doom.

The terror of the Day of the Lord, as Amos reinterprets it, may be heard tolling throughout his oracles, with its announcement of the inevitable, imminent and catastrophic climax of Israel's present way of life. 'In that day', the prophet declares, the warriors of the nation will be seized with panic and confusion,[14] the triumphant hymns of the sanctuary will turn to songs of lamentation,[15] an eclipse of the sun will darken the earth at noon,[16] and even the young and vigorous will faint.[17]

It is noteworthy that Amos never attempts a detailed description of the coming disaster. Exile is his usual term[18] and in declaring that God will raise up a nation to overrun

---

[13] *(contd.)*

'Amun hearkeneth unto me and cometh, when I cry to him. He stretched out his hand to me, and I rejoice; he calleth out behind me: 'Forward, forward! I am with thee, I thy father. Mine hand is with thee, and I am of more avail than a hundred thousand men, I, the lord of victory, that loveth strength.' I have found my courage again . . . I find that the two thousand five hundred chariots, in whose midst I was, lie hewn in pieces before my steeds. Not one of them hath found his hand to fight. Their hearts are become faint in their bodies for fear, their arms are all become powerless. They are unable to shoot, and have not the heart to take their lances . . . I shouted out to my army: 'Steady, steady your hearts, my soldiers. Ye behold my victory, I being alone. But Amun is my protector, and his hand is with me' (Adolf Erman, *The Ancient Egyptians*, trans. A. M. Blackman, pp. 260–70).

14. Amos 2. 14–16.
15. Amos 8. 3, 10.
16. Amos 8. 9.
17. Amos 8. 13.
18. Amos 5. 5, 27; 6. 7; 7. 11, 17.

the whole land he is almost certainly thinking of Assyria.[19]
But this is not the point: he is announcing the enemy action
not of any merely human power, but that of God himself:

> Therefore thus says the LORD, the God of hosts, the Lord:
> 'In all the squares there shall be wailing;
>   and in all the streets they shall say, "Alas! alas!"
> They shall call the farmers to mourning
>   and to wailing those who are skilled in lamentation,
> and in all vineyards there shall be wailing,
>   for *I will pass through the midst of you*,'
> says the LORD.[20]

It is a mistake, therefore, to read Amos' message as a theological interpretation of the international situation which
others might have explained in purely political terms, and
then to find in the eventual collapse of the northern kingdom
its approximate verification. For the prophet, Assyria was no
more than a convenient agent of God's judgement and the
cause of that judgement was so obvious in the corruption of
Israel's life as to require no confirmation from the imperial
ambitions of an external enemy.

The 'signs of the times' that Amos read were not political
but moral. God had become Israel's enemy for the simple
reason that Israelites had become enemies to each other.
Society was ravaged by greed and poisoned by injustice.
Amos' primary explanation of the coming judgement is the
outrageous oppression of the poor and defenceless:

> Hear this word, you cows of Bashan,
>   who are in the mountain of Samaria,
> who oppress the poor, who crush the needy,
>   who say to their husbands,
>   'Bring, that we may drink!'[21]

19. Amos 6. 14; cf. 3. 11.
20. Amos 5. 16, 17.
21. Amos 4. 1; cf. 2. 6–8; 3. 9, 10; 5. 11, 12; 8. 4–6.

The law courts afforded no redress for such victims of tyranny, since they themselves were riddled with bribery.[22] Self-interest was the ethic of Israel. It was self-interest which amassed the resources of the country for the ostentatious indulgence of the few[23] and guaranteed the prosperity of an established religion which was basically designed to secure good fortune for those who participated in its rituals.[24] Amos' indictment of the rich and of the religious is equally devastating.[25]

The criteria underlying the prophet's verdict are easy to identify but difficult to trace with confidence to their source. His basic concept is 'righteousness', which is known in the pursuit of 'justice' and identified with that 'good' which is ultimately synonymous with the will of God himself.[26] The sovereignty of God is the sovereignty of the good. For the familiar priestly exhortation to 'seek' God in the sanctuaries,[27] Amos defiantly substituted the demand that Israel should 'seek' God himself *outside the sanctuaries*: 'Seek me and live; but do not seek Bethel.'[28] It was moral obedience which gave access to God and to the security they desired:

> Seek good, and not evil,
>   that you may live;
> and so the LORD, the God of hosts,
>   will be with you,
>   as you have said.
> Hate evil, and love good,
>   and establish justice in the gate;
> it may be that the LORD, the God of hosts,
>   will be gracious to the remnant of Joseph.[29]

22. Amos 2. 7; 5. 7, 10–15; 6. 12.
23. Amos 3. 10, 15; 5. 11; 6. 4–6.
24. Amos 2. 8; 4. 4, 5.
25. Amos 5. 21–4.
26. Amos 5. 7, 24; 6. 12; see pp. 72–4.
27. Cf. Ps. 27. 8.
28. Amos 5. 4, 5.
29. Amos 5. 14, 15.

In his indictment both of the nations[30] and of Israel, Amos takes for granted generally recognized norms of human behaviour, so that it is enough for him to present the shameful facts without any reference to authoritative laws and precepts. His adoption of these moral norms as the touchstone of Israel's unique relationship with God was, however, inspired specifically by the covenant theology of his Mosaic heritage:

> Hear this word that the LORD has spoken against you, O people of Israel, against the whole family which I brought up out of the land of Egypt:

> 'You only have I known
>   of all the families of the earth;
> therefore I will punish you
>   for all your iniquities.'[31]

According to the Mosaic tradition, Israel owed its very existence as a historical people to a special relationship with God initiated by him in the Exodus from Egypt.[32] The character and continuation of that relationship were determined from the outset by the people's response to God's will (of which the Ten Commandments stood as the fundamental statement).[33] However, in the popular cult of the sanctuaries, the *conditional* character of the covenant had been obliterated in the clamour for religious assurance and, ironically, the Exodus deliverance itself had come to be interpreted as the irrevocable guarantee of God's favour to his Elect. It was this debased triumphalism that Amos violently demolished. The Exodus, he proclaimed in one of his most radical oracles, gave Israel no more security than was enjoyed by her enemies:

30. Amos 1. 3–2. 3.
31. Amos 3. 1, 2; cf. 2. 9, 10.
32. See pp. 102–3.
33. Exod. 20. 1–17.

'Are you not like the Ethiopians to me,
   O people of Israel?' says the LORD.
'Did I not bring up Israel from the land of Egypt,
   and the Philistines from Caphtor
   and the Syrians from Kir?
Behold, the eyes of the Lord GOD
   are upon the sinful kingdom,
and I will wipe it off the face of the earth.'[34]

How is this destruction of Israel to be understood? Elsewhere, Amos announces the plundering of Israel by an invading army[35] and the exile of the people.[36] It is impossible, of course, to translate the passionate poetry of prophetic invective into pedestrian prose, but we are clearly intended to conclude that the action is that of God himself as he brings his old relationship with Israel to an end:

'The end has come upon my people Israel;
I will never again pass by them.
The songs of the temple shall become
   wailings in that day,'
   says the Lord GOD;
'the dead bodies shall be many;
   in every place they shall be cast out in silence.'[37]

Apart from the oracles of 9. 11–15, which significantly reflect the royal theology of Jerusalem and are undoubtedly additions made by a later interpreter, the book of Amos is devoid of any word of promise for the future. Is it, then, equally devoid of hope? On one occasion, instead of the usual irrevocable decree, Amos employs a threat which enshrines an alternative to judgement:

34. Amos 9. 7, 8a; cf. 1. 3–5, 6–8.
35. Amos 3. 11; 5. 3; 6. 8, 14; 7. 9; 9. 4.
36. Amos 5. 5, 27; 6. 7; 7. 11, 17.
37. Amos 8. 2, 3; cf. 4. 12; 7. 9; 9. 1, 4.

Seek the LORD and live,
lest he break out like fire in the
   house of Joseph,
and it devour, with none to quench it.[38]

The possibility of Israel's returning to God is also contemplated in two further passages of exhortation[39] and God's
staying his judgement out of sheer grace ('It shall not be')
explicitly falls within the range of the prophet's thought.[40]
Obviously, the personal vocation of Amos would be more
intelligible if it were possible to interpret all his oracles as
simple threats, of which the 'either/or' offered the people a
straight choice; but this would be to go beyond the evidence.
'The end has come upon my people Israel' was, it seems, the
message he believed himself called to deliver.

Amos' legacy to the future – that future of Israel which
he seems to have denied (but about which the collectors of
his oracles evidently concluded that his words were not to
be taken literally) – was a passionate belief in God's moral
and universal sovereignty. His judgement of the nations,
extended inexorably to the judgement of Israel,[41] testified
to a historical order governed by a God of righteousness.
And that was to become the ground of Israel's faith in times
when its vision was darkened not by prosperity but by
suffering.

ISAIAH

The teaching of Isaiah of Jerusalem in the last half of the
eighth century BC rests on the single and uncompromising
conviction that God is supremely sovereign in history and
governs the nations of the world according to his own
determined plan:

38. Amos 5. 6.
39. Amos 5. 4, 5; 5. 14, 15.
40. Amos 7. 3, 6.
41. Amos 1. 3–2. 16.

The LORD of hosts has sworn:
'As I have planned,
  so shall it be,
and as I have purposed,
  so shall it stand,
that I will break the Assyrian in
  my land,
and upon my mountains trample
  him under foot;
and his yoke shall depart from them,
  and his burden from their shoulder.'
This is the purpose that is purposed
  concerning the whole earth;
and this is the hand that is
  stretched out
  over all the nations.
For the LORD of hosts has purposed,
  and who will annul it?
His hand is stretched out,
  and who will turn it back?[42]

What Isaiah requires from his people is the calm acceptance
of events as they occur, in the confidence that they have been
divinely ordained. It follows that the basic sin for Isaiah is
pride – the pride which refuses this serene faith and drives
people to engage in political activity, as though it were *their*
business to influence the course of history:

Oh, rebel sons! says the LORD,
you make plans, but not of my devising,
you weave schemes, but not inspired by me,
piling sin upon sin;
you hurry down to Egypt without consulting me,
to seek protection under Pharaoh's shelter
  and take refuge under Egypt's wing.[43]

42. Isa. 14. 24–7.
43. Isa. 30. 1, 2 (NEB); cf. 31. 1–3.

This majestic but terrifyingly simple theological position was maintained without change throughout a turbulent half-century of international politics, dominated, as it was, by the resurgence of the power of Assyria and the inauguration of its policy of conquering the smaller states of Syria and Palestine in a drive south towards Egypt. Isaiah lived to see the complete annexation of the northern kingdom[44] and Jerusalem's narrow escape from annihilation.[45] In each of the successive crises of his ministry,[46] Isaiah invariably presented Judah with a choice: *either* faith in God's providential ordering of events, *or* devastation and destruction. When, for example, in 734 BC, Ahaz rejected the prophet's demand that he should remain calm in the face of the threat from Rezin of Damascus and Pekah of Israel and faithlessly sought the protection of Assyria, Isaiah declared with unambiguous finality that it was by Assyria that Judah would be engulfed.[47] The same choice, the same refusal, and the same fate are encountered again at the end of Isaiah's ministry, when the political alignment had shifted and Judah was seeking the protection of Egypt against Assyria:

For thus said the Lord GOD, the Holy One of Israel,
'In returning and rest you shall be saved;
in quietness and in trust shall be your strength.'
And you would not, but you said,
  'No! We will speed upon horses,'
therefore you shall speed away;
  and, 'We will ride upon swift steeds,'
therefore your pursuers shall be swift.
A thousand shall flee at the threat of one,
  at the threat of five you shall flee,
till you are left

44. Isa. 28. 1–4.
45. Isa. 1. 7–9.
46. See p. 21.
47. Isa. 7. 1–9; 8. 5–8.

like a flagstaff on the top of a mountain,
like a signal on a hill.[48]

It was by rejecting the promise of salvation enshrined in the prophet's demand for faith that Judah brought upon itself complete and utter disaster.

Isaiah's oracles of judgement are as stark and uncompromising as those of Amos and no less resourceful in their invective. Jerusalem, he announces, will sink into impotent anarchy[49] and the Lord's vineyard become a waste land.[50] Judah is a wall, cracked by corruption, now to come crashing down, broken to bits:

Therefore thus says the Holy One of Israel,
'Because you despise this word,
    and trust in oppression and perverseness,
    and rely on them;
therefore this iniquity shall be to you
    like a break in a high wall, bulging
    out, and about to collapse,
    whose crash comes suddenly, in an instant;
and its breaking is like that of a potter's vessel
    which is smashed so ruthlessly
that among its fragments not a sherd is found
    with which to take fire from the hearth,
    or to dip up water out of the cistern.'[51]

Isaiah held that Assyria had been chosen as the agent of God's judgement,[52] but, like Amos, he was far from being motivated by political realism. Otherwise, he could never have proclaimed that even this imperial scourge of the nations would also be brought low, since it had arrogantly claimed an autonomy which denied the exclusive sovereignty of God:

48. Isa. 30. 15–17; cf. 28. 12.
49. Isa. 3. 1–7; 3. 24–4. 1.
50. Isa. 5. 1–7; cf. 7. 18–22; 32. 9–14.
51. Isa. 30. 12–14.
52. Isa. 7. 20; 10. 5, 6; 28. 11.

When the Lord has finished all his work on Mount Zion and on Jerusalem he will punish the arrogant boasting of the king of Assyria and his haughty pride. For he says:

'By the strength of my hand I have done it,
    and by my wisdom, for I have understanding;
I have removed the boundaries of peoples,
    and have plundered their treasures;
    like a bull I have brought down
    those who sat on thrones . . .'
Shall the axe vaunt itself over him
    who hews with it,
or the saw magnify itself against him who wields it?
As if a rod should wield him who lifts it,
    or as if a staff should lift him who is not wood![53]

With impeccable theological consistency but with not a trace of statesmanlike calculation, those nations which were actually the victims of Assyria's 'haughty pride' – Damascus, Philistia, Egypt[54] – are equally denounced for their scheming diplomacy.[55] It comes, therefore, as no surprise to learn that for Isaiah the Day of the Lord is not only a rejection of his own people, but a universal judgement on all who challenge the 'glory of his majesty':

The haughty looks of man shall be brought low,
    and the pride of men shall be humbled;
and the LORD alone will be exalted in that day.[56]

Isaiah's oracles are not very explicit about the positive criteria of the judgement they announce. Apart from the fundamental test of unreserved faith, to which all else is subordinated, Isaiah's moral norms are those of Amos. He condemns a

53. Isa. 10. 12, 13, 15; cf. 14. 24–7.
54. Isa. 17. 1–6; 14. 28–31; 18. 1–6; 20. 1–6.
55. Isa. 30. 1–5; 31. 1–3.
56. See Isa. 2. 6–22.

society in which the weak go to the wall,[57] the powerful lead lives of defiant debauchery,[58] and the cult flourishes,[59] as faith declines.[60]

It is even more difficult to identify the precise theological inspiration that underlies Isaiah's prophetic conviction. His oracles disclose no knowledge of the great affirmations of Mosaic faith, or of the familiar terms which expound God's intimate relationship with Israel (such as 'know', 'choose', 'love'). It is true that he speaks of Israel as God's 'sons'[61] and as a vineyard cared for by the Lord,[62] but both figures are more probably derived from the stock teaching of the schools than from the personal life of the family.[63] Characteristically, Isaiah talks about Judah coldly as 'this people';[64] it is hardly conceivable that he ever thought of God as Father. The nearest he gets to the sympathy and compassion of men like Amos, Hosea and Jeremiah is the recognition that God's rejection of his people is a strange and outlandish work,[65] and there is one moment of personal emotion which is unique in the record of his sayings:

That is why I said: Turn your eyes away from me;
leave me to weep in misery.
Do not press consolation on me
for the ruin of my people.[66]

Some scholars have advanced the view that Isaiah espoused the royal theology of Jerusalem, of which the central doctrines were God's unconditional covenant with the Davidic

57. Isa. 1. 21–3; 3. 14, 15; 5. 7, 8–10, 23; 10. 1, 2.
58. Isa. 2. 7; 3. 16, 17; 5. 11, 12; 9. 8–10; 28. 7–13; 32. 11.
59. Isa. 1. 10–17.
60. Isa. 5. 18, 19; 28. 9–13; 29. 13, 14; 30. 9–11.
61. Isa. 1. 2–4; 30. 9.
62. Isa. 5. 1–7.
63. See pp. 61–2, 99–100.
64. Isa. 6. 10; 8. 6, 11, 12; 9. 16; 28. 11, 14; 29. 13, 14.
65. Isa. 28. 21; 29. 14.
66. Isa. 22. 4 (REB).

dynasty[67] and his guarantee of the inviolability of Zion from all its enemies.[68] It is abundantly clear that the prophet's oracles were transmitted and reinterpreted in circles which were dominated by these doctrines,[69] but the primary tradition of Isaiah himself reveals little, if any, such influence. In the oracle of 22. 1–14, given when Jerusalem had escaped a damaging Assyrian siege, so far from invoking the dogma of Zion's inviolability to account for the deliverance, Isaiah denounced the city for its crass jubilation. For him, the attack was an act of God to win the people's repentance and their failure to respond to the deliverance was their own act of self-destruction. Similarly, his announcement of the annihilation of the City of David is a flat denial of all that the royal theology of Jerusalem affirmed:

> Woe betide Ariel! Ariel, the city where David encamped.
> When another year has passed,
> with its full round of pilgrim-feasts,
> then I shall reduce Ariel to sore straits.
> There will be moaning and lamentation
> when I make her my Ariel, my fire-altar.
> I shall encircle you with my army,
> set a ring of outposts all round you,
> and erect siege-works against you.[70]

There are two – and only two – oracles of promise for Zion which have a claim to come from Isaiah himself and both deny the traditional dogma of its inviolability. The first looks forward to the time when Jerusalem, purged by the fires of judgement, will be *renewed* and so become what its name implied:

> I will turn my hand against you
>   and will smelt away your dross as with lye

67. II Sam. 7. 4–17; Ps. 89. 1–4, 19–37; see pp. 141–2.
68. Ps. 46; 48. 1–8; 76. 1–6.
69. Isa. 4. 2–6; 9. 2–7; 10. 24–7; 11. 1–10; 17. 12–14; 29. 5, 7, 8; 31. 5, 9; 32. 1–5; 33. 17–20; 37. 33–5; 38. 5, 6.
70. Isa. 29. 1–3 (REB); cf. 8. 11–15, 16–18; 31. 4.

and remove all your alloy.
And I will restore your judges as at the first,
    and your counsellors as at the beginning.
Afterward you shall be called the city of righteousness,
    the faithful city.[71]

The second oracle promises that God will build a *new* sanctuary in Zion offering security on *new* conditions – faith, justice and righteousness:

Behold, I am laying in Zion for a foundation
    a stone, a tested stone,
a precious cornerstone, of a sure foundation:
'He who believes will not be in haste.'
And I will make justice the line,
    and righteousness the plummet.[72]

A further idea associated with the royal theology – the so-called doctrine of the remnant – belongs, similarly, to the secondary tradition of Isaiah's transmitters and interpreters.[73] Except for its occurrence in the ambiguous name *Shear-jashub*, where it seems to offer a threat that Judah would be reduced to a mere 'residue',[74] the term 'remnant' (*sheār*) represents the later claim of those who survived the fall of Jerusalem that they were the privileged few whom God intended to preserve.[75] This interpretation of the evidence finds support in the reflection that an announcement of the future survival of a *few* would never have provided more than cold comfort to the *many* and that it was only retrospectively that actual survivors (wise and confident after the event) could have contrived to make it a word of promise.

In relation to both of the major theological traditions of pre-exilic Israel – the Moses–Exodus tradition and the

71. Isa. 1. 25, 26.
72. Isa. 28. 16, 17.
73. Isa. 4. 3; 10. 20, 21; 11. 11, 16; 28. 5; 37. 31, 32.
74. Isa. 7. 3; cf. 8. 1–4, 18; see pp. 133–5.
75. Mic. 4. 6, 7; 5. 7–9; Zeph. 3. 11–13; Jer. 50. 20; see pp. 35–6.

David–Zion tradition – Isaiah's prophetic message is remarkably detached and uncommitted. It draws little from the heritage of God's dealing with Israel in the past and is tentative about their relationship in the future. His oracles are almost wholly preoccupied with the *present* and the present is always both a manifestation of God's inscrutable sovereignty and an invitation to accept it in total trust:

> For thus said the Lord GOD, the Holy One of Israel,
> 'In returning and rest you shall be saved;
> in quietness and in trust shall be your strength.'[76]

Time after time Israel is offered the choice;[77] time after time, Israel rejects God's rule and so brings upon itself rejection.[78] In its quietist emphasis on faith, the central theme of Isaiah's theology closely resembles the outlook to be found in the literature of Egypt's scribes, who similarly counsel a silent reliance on divine providence:

> Do not say, I have found a strong protector
>   And now I can challenge a man in my town.
> Do not say, I have found an active intercessor,
>   And now I can challenge him whom I hate.
>
> Indeed, you cannot know the plans of God;
>   You cannot perceive tomorrow.
> Sit yourself at the hands of God:
>   Your tranquillity will cause them to open.[79]

This similarity, together with his acquaintance with the literary forms familiar in the scribal schools,[80] lends support to the speculation that Isaiah was himself educated as an official. Further, his almost fanatical insistence that God

76. Isa. 30. 15; 7. 1–9; 28. 12.
77. Isa. 1. 18–20.
78. Isa. 6. 11–13.
79. The Instruction of Amen-em-ope, chapter 21, in *The Literature of Ancient Egypt*, ed. W. K. Simpson.
80. Isa. 1. 2, 3; 10. 15; 28. 23–9; 29. 15, 16; see pp. 61–3.

monopolizes the political arena[81] suggests that before his call to be a prophet, Isaiah had himself been one of those professional political counsellors, 'wise in their own eyes, and shrewd in their own sight',[82] whose expertise he repudiated, when, in his inaugural vision, he had seen 'the King, the Lord of Hosts'.[83]

MICAH

Micah, a younger contemporary of Isaiah who preached in Jerusalem about 725 BC,[84] is significant not because he says anything new, but because he confirms the existence of an established tradition of prophetic teaching in pre-exilic Israel and presents it with unequalled vigour. He shared the moral norms of Amos and Isaiah and reaffirmed their indictment of a society corrupted by the power of wealth and the exploitation of the ordinary citizen. A man could no longer call his home his own[85] and his family lived in fear.[86] The protection afforded by the courts, once everybody's birthright, was now a black market commodity open to the biggest bribe.[87] In Micah's affluent society, only human life was cheap:

> Hear, you heads of Jacob
>   and rulers of the house of Israel!
> Is it not for you to know justice? –
>   you who hate the good and love the evil,
>   who tear the skin from off my people,
>   and their flesh from off their bones;
> who eat the flesh of my people,
>   and flay their skin from off them,

81. Isa. 30. 1–5; 31. 1–3.
82. Isa. 5. 21.
83. Isa. 6. 5.
84. For a critical analysis of the book of Micah, see pp. 16–17.
85. Mic. 2. 1, 2; cf. Hos. 5. 10; Isa. 5. 8–10; Prov. 23. 10.
86. Mic. 2. 8, 9; cf. Amos 5. 11.
87. Mic. 3. 9–11; cf. Amos 2. 7; 5. 7, 10–13, 15; 6. 12; Isa. 5. 7, 23.

and break their bones in pieces,
   and chop them up like meat in a kettle,
   like flesh in a cauldron.[88]

The leaders of Israel – elders, priests and institutional prophets – were no more than ringleaders in its social disintegration.[89] The ranting prophets promised prosperity for tips[90] and the people were well satisfied with their smooth assurances: 'Is not the LORD in the midst of us? No evil shall come upon us.'[91]

With the courageous conviction of that radically different kind of prophecy which emerged with Amos, Micah declares the inescapable destruction of the whole intolerable brood,[92] which by its inhumanity had ceased to be God's people and become, instead, his enemy: 'But you are no people for me, rising up as my enemy to my face.'[93] Like the sophisticated and idolatrous city of Samaria,[94] 'the hill-shrine of Judah' (as Micah contemptuously calls Jerusalem)[95] would be razed to the ground:

Therefore, on your account
Zion shall become a ploughed field,
Jerusalem a heap of ruins,
   and the temple hill rough heath.[96]

A century later, when Jeremiah repeated this blasphemous denial of Zion's inviolability, Micah's words, it is said, were remembered.[97]

---

88. Mic. 3. 1–3; cf. Amos 6. 4–7; 8. 4–6; Isa. 3. 14, 15.
89. Mic. 3. 11.
90. Mic. 2. 6; 3. 5–7; cf. Isa. 30. 9–11; Ezek. 13. 17–19.
91. Mic. 3. 11; 2. 7; cf. Amos 5. 14; 6. 1–3; 9. 10.
92. Mic. 2. 3.
93. Mic. 2. 8 (NEB); cf. Amos 5. 18–20.
94. Mic. 1. 6, 7.
95. Mic. 1. 5 (NEB).
96. Mic. 3. 12 (NEB).
97. Jer. 26. 18.

CHAPTER 6

Salvation Through Judgement

HOSEA

Hosea's prophetic ministry is best understood as a quest for the recovery of Israel's identity. Other prophets represent themselves as messengers sent by God; Hosea is scarcely distinguishable from the God for whom he speaks. This impression of unmediated divine address is partly due to the almost total absence from his book of oracle formulae like 'Thus saith the Lord' (4.1 and 5.1 being notable exceptions) and to the fusion of his individual sayings into loose thematic complexes presented in the first person as the personal discourse of God himself.[1] In the final analysis, however, this directness of speech depends on the highly personal quality of the prophet's language. Like a good actor, Hosea does not merely mouth his lines; he lives his part. And since his part as prophet was created by a knowledge of God so authenticating as to remove all doubt and ambiguity,[2] he was free to be himself and say what he thought.

Hosea's language is an astonishingly fresh and informal re-presentation of Israel's Mosaic faith.[3] For Amos of the southern kingdom, the saving history of the Exodus and Conquest was so identified with complacent religious assurance as to demand that he should totally repudiate it. For Hosea, however, the only independent prophet from the northern kingdom, God's history with Israel was seen as affording his contemporaries their only hope and means of deliverance from the alien morass into which they had

---

1. Hos. 2. 2–15; 4. 1–14; 5. 1–13; 11. 1–11.
2. Cf. Hos. 6. 6; 4. 6; 13. 4.
3. Hos. 12. 13.

allowed themselves to sink. That is why he dwells on the Exodus from Egypt,[4] God's protection of his people in the Wilderness,[5] and his gift of the land of Palestine.[6] His purpose, however, is not merely to affirm what God had done for his people in the past, but to make them aware of what God is doing in the present – because of what he is and always has been:

> I am the LORD your God
>   from the land of Egypt;
> you know no God but me,
>   and besides me there is no saviour.
> It was I who knew you in the wilderness.[7]

God's historical dealings with Israel disclose, for Hosea, his character as a person and the personal character of his relations with his people. Hosea's greatest achievement is to have penetrated the personal core of Mosaic faith and to have presented with complete spontaneity the history of Israel with its God as the story of a family relationship:

> When Israel was a boy, I loved him;
>   I called my son out of Egypt;
> but the more I called, the further they went from me;
>   they must needs sacrifice to the Baalim
>   and burn offerings before carved images.
> It was I who taught Ephraim to walk,
>   I who had taken them in my arms;
> but they did not know that I harnessed them in leading-strings
>   and led them with bonds of love –
> that I had lifted them like a little child to my cheek,
>   that I had bent down to feed them.[8]

---

4. Hos. 2. 14, 15; 11. 1; 12. 9; 13. 4.
5. Hos. 9. 10; 13. 5.
6. Hos. 9. 3; cf. 2. 8.
7. Hos. 13. 4, 5.
8. Hos. 11. 1–4 (NEB).

This supremely sensitive vignette of Israel as God's son, lifted up as a child to his father's cheek, fed and taught to walk by him, discloses a deep awareness that a relationship between persons is the appropriate analogy for the reality of Israel's faith. That is why Hosea's parallel figure of the husband and wife, though bold in view of the sexual elements in Canaanite ritual practice, requires no different explanation.[9]

For Hosea, Israel's identity as a people was a personal identity – created and sustained by its relationship to the personal God. Apart from this, it was nothing and it was a 'worthless nothing' it had chosen to become.[10] Israel had forfeited its very being and it was Hosea's mission to win it back to its true self.[11] This meant that it must be extricated from two alien spheres – the Canaanite cult, which dominated Israel's sanctuaries, and the power game of international politics, in which the secularized northern monarchy was dabbling to its ruin.

The Canaanite cult was designed for fertility and operated through sexual rites and similar acts of sympathetic magic calculated to coerce the forces of nature. Hosea's passionate indictment of this 'harlotry',[12] though not without its moral content,[13] is directed primarily at the false allegiance it disclosed. Israel simply had no existence in connection with Baal;[14] its very identity as a people depended on its relationship to the God of the Exodus, who not only created it in the beginning, but still sustained it.[15] Israel was not a child of nature, but a child of history and through history a child of God.[16] The exploitation of human sexuality in a sub-personal cult is a horrible caricature[17] of the true relationship between

9. Hos. 1. 2–2. 17; 3. 1–5.
10. Hos. 8. 8; cf. 5. 11.
11. Hos. 4. 10–12; 9. 10; 13. 6.
12. Hos. 2. 2, 4, 5; 3. 1; 4. 13, 14; 6. 10; 9. 1.
13. Cf. Hos. 4. 1, 2; 6. 8, 9; 7. 1–4; 10. 4; 12. 7, 8.
14. Hos. 7. 16; see p. 40.
15. Hos. 2. 8; 7. 15.
16. Hos. 11. 1–11.
17. Hos. 6. 10.

men and women, which for the prophet (as for St Paul eight centuries later) is so profound a mystery as to serve as a model for God's relations with his people.[18]

Just as Israel, if it were to regain its true identity, must be extricated from its involvement with the religion of the surrounding nations, so it must be pulled out of their power politics. It is this conviction which underlies Hosea's condemnation of the Israelite monarchy[19] and of the conspiracies and alliances upon which it depended.[20] In the political chaos that broke out in the northern kingdom shortly after Hosea began his ministry in about 750 BC and which threw up no less than six kings (of whom certainly four were murdered) in a mere twenty years,[21] the prophet must have found much to confirm his conviction that the power game was a parody of God's purpose for his people:

> Israel is now swallowed up,
> lost among the nations,
>   a worthless nothing.[22]

Whereas Isaiah coldly condemned political activity as the arrogant rejection of God's sovereignty, Hosea simply lost his temper.[23] He 'poured out his wrath like a flood'[24] at the spectacle of God's crazy son[25] going careering off among the nations like a wild ass,[26] or a silly, senseless pigeon,[27] obtusely unaware of what he was forsaking and of the cruel fate awaiting him.[28]

Hosea had no illusions about the disaster confronting his contemporaries and held out no hope of its being averted:

18. Hos. 1. 2–2. 17; 3. 1–5; cf. Eph. 5. 25–33.
19. Hos. 1. 4; 7. 3–7; 8. 4; 10. 13–15; 13. 10, 11.
20. Hos. 5. 13; 7. 8, 9, 11; 8. 9, 10; 12. 1.
21. II Kgs. 15. 8–31.
22. Hos. 8. 8 (NEB).
23. Cf. Hos. 8. 5; see p. 106.
24. Hos. 5. 10; 13. 11.
25. Hos. 11. 2.
26. Hos. 8. 9; cf. 4. 16.
27. Hos. 7. 11.
28. Hos. 7. 9.

> The days of punishment have come,
>   the days of recompense have come;
> Israel shall know it.[29]

The ravaging of the northern kingdom by Assyria in 733 BC was the unalterable doom proclaimed by God himself[30] and the coming destruction of its capital city of Samaria would be no less his work of judgement on his people's ungrateful rebellion.[31]

This preaching is no conventional theological interpretation of a fate that was seen to be politically inevitable, in order to salvage out of the disaster some sort of belief in God's control of history; so much is abundantly clear from the uninhibited violence of Hosea's language. Having unsuccessfully lashed Israel and torn it to shreds through the prophets,[32] having made himself a festering sore and canker on its loathsome body,[33] God, Hosea proclaims, will now maul his people as a panther his prey,[34] and meet them like a she-bear robbed of her cubs and tear their ribs apart.[35] Paradoxically, the very anger that seethes through these images of God's action points to the ground of Israel's hope, since they convey that sense of personal outrage inseparable from genuine caring.[36] The vitality of the language springs from the vitality of God's relationship with his people.[37] Because for Hosea (in contrast to Amos) this relationship has a dimension that transcends even the sacred obligations of morality, it cannot be broken by sin:

> How can I give you up, O Ephraim!
> How can I hand you over, O Israel!

29. Hos. 9. 7; cf. 4. 5; 5. 9.
30. Hos. 5. 8–14.
31. Hos. 13. 4–16.
32. Hos. 6. 5.
33. Hos. 5. 12.
34. Hos. 5. 14.
35. Hos. 13. 8.
36. Hos. 5. 3; 13. 4, 5.
37. Hos. 7. 1, 2.

How can I make you like Admah!
How can I treat you like Zeboiim!
My heart recoils within me,
my compassion grows warm and tender.
I will not execute my fierce anger,
I will not again destroy Ephraim;
for I am God and not man,
the Holy One in your midst,
and I will not come to destroy.[38]

It is impossible to judge with confidence how Hosea envisaged the realization of this promise, since some of the more explicit passages are probably later editorial additions.[39] In the analogy of his redeeming love for his faithless wife, it is the discipline of exile that will move Israel to respond to God's open invitation to return.[40] The inclusion of Egypt with Assyria as the place of exile almost certainly reflects the historical situation,[41] but possibly it also reflects Hosea's view that the penalty must correspond to the offence, since, so far from being retributive, it is educational and remedial: 'Ephraim is a silly, senseless pigeon, now calling upon Egypt, now turning to Assyria for help.'[42]

In the promise of 2. 14, 15, however, the emphasis falls exclusively on God's personal initiative: like a forsaken husband,[43] he will woo Israel into making an entirely fresh start from the original point of departure:

Therefore, behold, I will allure her,
and bring her into the wilderness,
and speak tenderly to her.
And there I will give her her vineyards,
and make the Vale of Trouble [Achor] into a Gate of Hope.

38. Hos. 11. 8, 9.
39. Hos. 1. 10–2. 1; 2. 16–23; 11. 10, 11.
40. Hos. 3. 1–5; cf. 2. 6, 7; 5. 15.
41. Hos. 7. 16; 8. 13; 9. 3, 6; 11. 5; cf. 11. 10, 11.
42. Hos. 7. 11 (NEB); cf. 12. 1.
43. Cf. Judg. 19. 3.

And there she shall answer as in the days of her youth,
as at the time when she came out of the land of Egypt.[44]

It is unnecessary to suppose that the threats and promises
of Hosea represent either a change of mind over the years
or a permanent state of indecision and unresolved conflict.
They disclose, rather, the complementary facets of a relationship founded on love[45] – a love which is no less
vulnerable and no less stringent because it is divine. By
being drawn into the personal reality of God's covenant
with Israel and by discovering there the very grounds of its
identity as a people in history, Hosea was able both to
comprehend the depths of Israel's alienation and to tran-
scend its devastating consequences.

JEREMIAH

Jeremiah was active as a prophet during the last harrowing
decades of the southern kingdom and experienced the fall of
Jerusalem in 587 BC. His oracles were taken over and reinterpreted by scribal teachers during the Exile that followed and
it is to them that most of the prose sections of the book may
be attributed. The task of rediscovering from this material the
mind of the prophet himself would be greatly simplified if the
poetic oracles could be accepted as the primary tradition and
the prose discourses relegated to the secondary tradition, but
such a division offers no more than a very general guide.

There is no doubt, however, that the unique series of
lamentations, the so-called confessions, in which Jeremiah
reveals his spiritual struggles with unprecedented candour,
provide wholly reliable evidence of his distinctive outlook.[46]
It is immediately evident that Jeremiah regards himself as a
man doomed to 'proclaim violence and destruction'[47] to a

44. Cf. Josh. 7. 20–6.
45. Hos. 3. 1.
46. Jer. 11. 18–23; 12. 1–6; 15. 10–12, 15–21; 17. 14–18; 18. 19–23; 20. 7–11,
14–18.
47. Jer. 20. 8; cf. 15. 10, 17; 17. 16.

people who are obdurately unresponsive,[48] but with whom, despite their hostility, he feels a profound sympathy and solidarity.[49] He finds the burden of God's prophetic commission almost beyond human endurance,[50] although he submits to it in agonized obedience.[51]

The contrast between Jeremiah's doubt – doubt about God's purpose and doubt about his own integrity – and the confidence of Amos, Isaiah and Micah could hardly be greater. These earlier prophets were sustained by that direct simplicity of conviction which has always been the layman's contribution to the People of God and their proclamation of God's unmitigated judgement was a response to the prosperous assurance of their age. Jeremiah, however, was a more complicated and, by upbringing, a more conventionally pious person, living in a period of unprecedented uncertainty. His experience compelled him to accept the role of God's independent 'assayer and tester' of his people,[52] but he undertook the task with reluctance and discharged it without zest.[53]

In the death throes of Jerusalem, it was hard for a sensitive man to speak with dogmatic assurance about God's righteous judgement and the strain of Jeremiah's public office is disclosed in the confidences of his private diary. These confidences are the work of a remarkable poet and their tortured questioning and black despair are reflected also in his public utterances:

> How can I bear my sorrow?
>   I am sick at heart.
> Hark, the cry of my people
>   from a distant land:
> 'Is the LORD not in Zion?
>   Is her King no longer there?'

48. Jer. 11. 19; 15. 10; 17. 18; 18. 22, 23.
49. Jer. 18. 20; cf. 4. 8; 8. 14.
50. Jer. 15. 17, 18; 17. 17; 20. 14–18.
51. Jer. 11. 20; 20. 7–9; see pp. 50–3.
52. Jer. 6. 27; 9. 7.
53. Jer. 1. 4–10.

Why do they provoke me with their images
    and foreign gods?
Harvest is past, summer is over,
    and we are not saved.
I am wounded at the sight of my people's wound;
    I go like a mourner, overcome with horror.[54]

It scarcely seems appropriate to classify many of Jeremiah's poems as prophetic oracles, since the formal structures of prophetic speech have been dissolved in more fluid discourses and their content has moved from denunciation and judgement to description and exhortation.[55]

In the latter respect, as in others, the similarity to Hosea is so close as to suggest direct dependence. Like his predecessor, Jeremiah contrasts that history which God had intended for his people with their horrifying desertion to foreign cults[56] and foreign alliances,[57] and he describes both in the personal language characteristic of Hosea. Israel became God's bride in the wilderness, but has gone off in search of other lovers;[58] God's own sons have now taken to crooked ways,[59] and are so possessed by what Hosea called 'the spirit of harlotry'[60] that they are totally unable to return.[61] The question that had agonized Hosea – 'How can I forgive you for all this?' – is taken up once again,[62] and once again it is followed by violent wild beast imagery to describe the inevitable punishment.[63] Jeremiah's own word for Judah's loss of her true identity is 'falsehood'.

The contrast between reality and delusion, truth and falsehood, dominates his prophecy and is an important key

54. Jer. 8. 18–21 (NEB); cf. 4. 19, 31; 9. 2, 3; 13. 15–17; 23. 9.
55. Jer. 2. 1–13; 3. 1–5; 5. 20–9; 12. 15–19.
56. Jer. 1. 16; 2. 8–13, 23–8; 13. 27.
57. Jer. 2. 18, 36.
58. Jer. 2. 1–13; 3. 1–5.
59. Jer. 3. 19, 20.
60. Hos. 4. 12.
61. Jer. 2. 20–2; 8. 4–6; 9. 5; 13. 23.
62. Jer. 5. 7, 9, 29; 9. 9; cf. Hos. 6. 4.
63. Jer. 5. 6.

to his thought. Like his predecessors in the previous century, he too, is incensed by injustice and profligacy, but he particularizes about very few of Judah's failings. He is distinctive, rather, for his deep psychological penetration and for his despairing conviction that the whole of Judah's life is permeated by falsehood: 'Falsehood and not truth has grown strong in the land.'[64] It is *truth* that God looks for, but in refusing to know him, they have lost their hold on reality.[65] The Hebrew word *sheqer*, meaning lie and falsehood, is used in the Old Testament rather more than a hundred times and no less than a third of these occurrences are found in the book of Jeremiah. Everywhere he looked, he found nothing but lies:

> Every one deceives his neighbour,
>   and no one speaks the truth;
> They have taught their tongue to speak lies;
>   they commit iniquity and are too weary to repent.[66]

The falsehood of the people's idolatrous cults is equalled only by the false security engendered by their idolatrous attitude to the Temple. The priests conspire with the prophets to promote this falsehood, promising that all is well.[67]

Jeremiah's task was to warn his contemporaries that they were living in a fool's paradise and, in his later years, to urge them to look for the hand of God not (as they all did) in the fall of Babylon, but in the fall of their own holy city:

> Learn your lesson, Jerusalem,
>   lest my love for you be torn from my heart,
>   and I leave you desolate,
>   a land where no one can live.[68]

64. Jer. 9. 3.

65. Jer. 2. 8; 4. 22; 5. 4, 5; 8. 7; 9. 1–6.

66. Jer. 9. 5; cf. 3. 23; 13. 25.

67. Jer. 5. 2, 30, 31; 6. 13, 14; 7. 1–15; 23. 17; 27. 10, 14, 16; 28. 1–4; 29. 9, 21, 23, 31; see pp. 34, 101.

68. Jer. 6. 8 (NEB).

In teaching this lesson to the bitter end, Jeremiah suffered intolerably. Worse even than being 'wounded at the sight of my people's wound', he was tormented by the suspicion that God had actually duped him,[69] so that it was he and not his opponents who was deceived.[70] Jeremiah had hoped against hope that the disaster would be averted by his people's change of heart.[71] When that hope was finally disappointed, it demanded superhuman courage to accept that God had, in fact, 'accomplished and fulfilled his deep designs'.[72]

It is in having become the personal embodiment of Israel's Mosaic faith during the course of the most threatening crisis of its history that Jeremiah's true greatness lies. His specific contribution to his people's hope for the future is to be found not so much in any words of promise which may be ascribed to him, as in the inspiration and opportunity he gave to those scribal teachers who developed and interpreted his work during the exilic period. Their outlook is closely akin to that which is found in Deuteronomy and I and II Kings, so that the prose tradition of the book, which is largely their work, consistently explains that the fall of Jerusalem was not (as the exiles were tempted to suppose) a defeat for God, but, rather, his deliberate and righteous act of judgement on his people's disobedience:

> And when your people say, 'Why has the LORD our God done all these things to us?' you shall say to them, 'As you have forsaken me and served foreign gods in your land, so you shall serve strangers in a land that is not yours.'[73]

If the exiles would accept disaster as God's righteous judgement, respond in penitence and return to him, he would be faithful to his promise and restore them to their

69. Jer. 20. 7; cf. 15. 18.
70. Jer. 28. 11; cf. 5. 12, 13.
71. Jer. 13. 15–17; 17. 16; 18. 20.
72. Jer. 23. 20.
73. Jer. 5. 19; 9. 12–16; 16. 10–13; 22. 8, 9; cf. Deut. 29. 21–3; I Kgs. 9. 8, 9.

own land.[74] Thus Israel's judgement could become the means of its salvation.

This teaching is presented not only in the prose discourses, but also in the narrative sections of the book. It is impossible to determine how much historical tradition underlies these narratives, but, for example, it is clear that the account of Jeremiah's deliberate purchase of the family property at Anathoth has been developed as a didactic story to support the discourse which follows[75]:

> Behold, I will gather them from all the countries to which I drove them in my anger and my wrath and in great indignation; I will bring them back to this place, and I will make them dwell in safety. And they shall be my people, and I will be their God. I will give them one heart and one way, that they may fear me for ever, for their own good and the good of their children after them. I will make with them an everlasting covenant, that I will not turn away from doing good to them; and I will put the fear of me in their hearts, that they may not turn from me. I will rejoice in doing them good, and I will plant them in this land in faithfulness, with all my heart and all my soul.[76]

This affirmation parallels the celebrated promise of the New Covenant and it is probable that in its present form this, too, is part of the later teachers' exposition of the prophet's message:

> Behold, the days are coming, says the LORD, when I will make a new covenant with the house of Israel and the house of Judah, not like the covenant which I made with their fathers when I took them by the hand to bring them out of the land of Egypt, my covenant which they broke, though I was their

74. Jer. 18. 7–10; 24. 4–7; 29. 10–14; 30. 2, 3; 31. 27–30; cf. Deut. 4. 25–31; 20. 1–6; I Kgs. 8. 46–53; II Kgs. 17. 7–23; 21. 10–15.
75. Jer. 32. 6–15.
76. Jer. 32. 37–41.

husband, says the LORD. But this is the covenant which I will
make with the house of Israel after those days, says the LORD:
I will put my law within them, and I will write it upon their
hearts; and I will be their God, and they shall be my people.
And no longer shall each man teach his neighbour and each
his brother, saying, 'Know the LORD', for they shall all know
me, from the least of them to the greatest, says the LORD; for
I will forgive their iniquity, and I will remember their sin no
more.[77]

The gracious initiative of God at the heart of this New
Covenant will empower his people to regain their true identity
in a relationship to him which will now be spontaneous. This
reflects an insight which seems to derive from the faith of
Jeremiah himself, since it goes beyond the deuteronomic
teachers' familiar exhortation to repent and explicitly contrasts the new covenant with the old – 'the covenant which I
made with their fathers when I took them . . . out of the land
of Egypt'.[78] Fundamentally, it is a restatement of Hosea's
understanding of that divine love which is able to conquer
without coercion and makes available a power that is equal
to all its demands.

77. Jer. 31. 31–4; cf. 24. 7.
78. Although the enabling grace of God is envisaged by the deuteronomic
teachers in Deut. 30. 6, characteristically, they urge that Israel must take the
initiative of 'turning again' before God's forgiveness may be received (cf. Deut.
4. 29–31; 30. 1–5; I Kgs. 8. 46–50).

CHAPTER 7

Salvation After Judgement

After the fall of Jerusalem in 587 BC, Nebuchadrezzar deported to Babylon the cream of Judah's population. Once in exile, many of the Jews settled down among the Babylonians as Jeremiah had advised them to do.[1] Others kept themselves separate from the society of their conquerors and prepared for their return to their own land. These were the people who determined the form of post-exilic Judaism and to a very large extent the final shape of the Old Testament. Between these two groups, the settlers and the separatists, there must have been a great number of Jews who were simply bewildered:

> Why do you say, O Jacob,
>   and speak, O Israel,
> 'My way is hid from the LORD,
>   and my right is disregarded by my God'?[2]

The peril of disillusionment, which threatened every national religion in the ancient world when it came up against adverse political fortune, was the problem that had to be faced after the shock of the deportation to Babylon. Like the women who told Jeremiah that they were reverting to the worship of the Queen of Heaven, because the prophetic faith of Israel had failed to provide what they wanted,[3] many of the exiles must previously have thought of their religious practice as an insurance policy against national disaster.[4] They too had been disillusioned. The policy did not cover 'acts of God'.

1. Jer. 29. 5–7, 27, 28; cf. Neh. 1. 11; 2. 1–8; Ezra 2. 68, 69; Ezek. 8. 1; 14. 1; 20. 1; 24. 18.
2. Isa. 40. 27; cf. 42. 22–4; 49. 14.
3. Jer. 44. 18.
4. Jer. 7. 9, 10.

There is little wonder that the national religions of Moab, Ammon, and the rest simply fizzled out when they failed to pass this exacting test. As the gods of the nations, it would appear, were scarcely more than personifications of social solidarity and national independence, they were inevitably discarded when their territories were absorbed into the great empires on their borders. The God of Israel was not forgotten in this way, because he continued to confront his people with judgement and mercy, through the events of history as interpreted by his servants the prophets.

SECOND ISAIAH

The anonymous poet of Isaiah 40–55 delivered his oracles at one of the most critical periods in the history not only of Israel but of the whole ancient Near East, when the era of the great Semitic empires was drawing to its close. Already the armies of Cyrus were victoriously extending the bounds of the Persian Empire,[5] and the collapse of Babylon, where the Jews were held in exile, was imminent. Second Isaiah rises to this tremendous occasion and with incomparable vision expounds the expected deliverance in the total context of God's purpose for Israel and, through Israel, for the world. Few historical scenes have ever been given so luminous a frame.

It is strange to reflect that Second Isaiah would almost certainly have been classed as an institutional prophet like Hananiah, and rejected as falsely promising salvation, if he had preached in Jeremiah's hearing only sixty years earlier.[6] The fact that he is now generally regarded as the last (and, by some, as the greatest) of the independent prophets illustrates the truth that it is not simply what a prophet says which counts, but the circumstances in which he says it. Because the theology of prophecy is fundamentally a theology of history, it is inescapably 'situational'. When Jeremiah spoke, Jerusalem was complacently refusing to recognize the reality of Babylonian

5. Isa. 44. 28; 45. 1.
6. Jer. 28. 1–16; see p. 36.

power and accept the divine judgement of Israel, of which he declared it was the instrument. When Second Isaiah spoke, Jerusalem was in ruins and its citizens (or more probably their descendants), now exiled in Babylon, were faithlessly refusing to recognize the reality of *God's* power and accept the deliverance of Israel, of which he declared the divine judgement of Babylon was the inauguration. If the basic criterion of independent prophecy is its speaking out on behalf of God in opposition to current opinion, in order to reaffirm in times of crisis his righteous, personal and invincible purpose, then Second Isaiah is a true successor of Jeremiah. Like him, he suffered the burdensome consequences of his calling:

> The Lord GOD opened my ears
>   and I did not disobey or turn back in defiance.
> I offered my back to the lash,
>   and let my beard be plucked from my chin,
> I did not hide my face from spitting and insult;
>   but the Lord GOD stands by to help me;
>   therefore no insult can wound me.
> I have set my face like flint,
>   for I know that I shall not be put to shame,
>   because one who will clear my name is at my side.
> Who dare argue against me? Let us confront one another.
> Who will dispute my cause? Let him come forward.[7]

The character and persistence of the opposition with which Second Isaiah had to contend emerge very clearly from the forms he adopted for his teaching. His *oracles of salvation* are modelled on the traditional cultic assurance given in the sanctuary in reply to laments such as were made either by individuals or by the community,[8] and his *polemical forms* (scenes from law court procedures[9] and from the schools[10])

---

7. Isa. 50. 5–8 (NEB); cf. 49. 4; 52. 13–53. 12; see pp. 50–3, 124.
8. Isa. 41. 8–13; 41. 14–16; 43. 1–4; 43. 5–7; 44. 1–5.
9. Isa. 41. 1–5; 41. 21–9; 43. 8–13; 44. 6–8, 21, 22; 45. 20–5.
10. Isa. 40. 12–17; 40. 18–26; 40. 27–31; 45. 9–13; 55. 8–11.

show the prophet fighting a whole battery of false accusations. In the oracles of salvation, the basic assurance 'Fear not'[11] counters the exiles' laments that God had cast them off,[12] left them in the lurch,[13] kept quiet and done nothing,[14] betrayed the promises he gave in the Exodus deliverance,[15] and sold them into tyranny.[16] This picture of a shattered and despairing community is confirmed by Second Isaiah's polemical forms. In the trial speeches and disputations, God defends himself against the charge that he has neither the will nor the power to help his people,[17] that his plans are untrustworthy[18] and that he has repudiated the covenant.[19]

The faith of the exilic community was threatened, however, not only by this kind of disillusionment about their God, but by the new and exciting alternatives offered by the gods of Babylon. It is for this reason that refutations of the claims of Babylonian religion dominate chapters 40–8 of the book. Even if the satires on idols and their makers derive, as seems probable, from a secondary tradition,[20] Second Isaiah's anxious concern about the gods of Babylon is clear enough:

Come, open your plea, says the LORD,
present your case, says Jacob's King;
let these idols come forward
and foretell the future for us.
Let them declare the meaning of these past events
that we may reflect on it;
let them predict the future to us
that we may know what it holds.

11. Isa. 41. 10, 14; 43. 1, 5; 54. 4; cf. Lam. 3. 57.
12. Isa. 41. 8–13, 14–16.
13. Isa. 41. 17–20.
14. Isa. 42. 14–17.
15. Isa. 43. 16–21.
16. Isa. 49. 7–12.
17. Isa. 40. 12–31; 44. 6–8; 45. 20–5.
18. Isa. 45. 9–13.
19. Isa. 50. 1–3.
20. Isa. 40. 19, 20; 41. 6, 7; 44. 9–20; 45. 16, 17; 46. 5–7.

Declare what is yet to happen;
then we shall know you are gods.
Do something, whether good or bad,
anything that will strike us with dismay and fear.
You cannot! You are sprung from nothing,
your works are non-existent.
To choose you is outrageous![21]

The trial speeches resound with God's curiously direct claims to sole divinity – 'I am the first and I am the last; besides me there is no god',[22] of which the form and the abstract content betray their derivation from Babylonian religious language.[23]

Second Isaiah is also indebted to the opposition for the basic premise of his arguments against the gods of Babylon, namely, that the ability to predict the future is the criterion of divinity.[24] He counters the Babylonians' claims in passionate declarations that it was not their gods, nor their associated astrologers, who could foretell future events, but the God of Israel;[25] he it was who knew the future, because the future, like all history, was created by his will and directed by his purpose:

Remember this and consider,
   recall it to mind, you transgressors,
   remember the former things of old;
for I am God, and there is no other;
   I am God, and there is none like me,
declaring the end from the beginning
   and from ancient times things not yet done,
saying, 'My counsel shall stand,
   and I will accomplish all my purpose,'
calling a bird of prey from the east,
   the man of my counsel from a far country.

21. Isa. 41. 21–4 (REB); cf. 43. 8–13; 44. 6–8, 21, 22; 45. 20–5.
22. Isa. 44. 6; 41. 4; 43. 10–12; 45. 21; cf. 45. 5, 6, 18; 46. 9; 48. 12.
23. Cf. Isa. 47. 8, 10.
24. Isa. 41. 21–4; 44. 7, 8; 45. 21; cf. 48. 14.
25. Isa. 47. 12, 13.

I have spoken, and I will bring it to pass;
I have purposed, and I will do it.[26]

Religious apologetic is always in danger of making compromising claims and here we find Second Isaiah exploiting for apologetic purposes the Babylonians' elaborate cultivation of the pseudo-science of divination and their obsession with secret knowledge of the future. To argue that it was the God of Israel who revealed 'the end from the beginning' was to run the risk of associating the independent prophets' belief about divine *sovereignty* with the institutional prophets' claim that they had access to divine *foreknowledge*.[27]

Unlike the professional soothsayers upon whom they lavished some of their very best vituperation,[28] the independent prophets did not believe that the future was determined in the immutable way that prediction necessarily demands. Whether in their declarations of doom, or (as with Second Isaiah) in their proclamations of salvation, their purpose was not to predict the future but to shape it, by eliciting the people's loyal response. The danger of the *Old Moore's Almanack* idea of the prophet's function, to which Second Isaiah appears to have lent his authority,[29] became fully apparent in the post-exilic community, when prophetic proclamation came to be reinterpreted as predictive knowledge and, ultimately, as a body of 'mysteries' from which the apocalyptic seers claimed to unlock 'the secrets of the future to the end of time'.[30]

It was, however, with the exiles' actual situation in history that Second Isaiah himself was concerned. The whole of his work is a vehement striving to conquer their doubt and despair through a renewal of faith in God's purpose for them.

26. Isa. 46. 8–11; cf. 41. 1–5, 25–9; 42. 16, 17; 43. 11–13; 45. 1–7; 48. 3–8, 12–16.

27. I Sam. 2. 34 (cf. 4. 11); 3. 19; 9. 5–9; II Sam. 12. 13–19; 1 Kgs. 14. 12–18; 21. 19 (cf. 22. 38).

28. See p. 37.

29. Isa. 44. 26; 48. 3; cf. Deut. 18. 20–2.

30. See pp. 157–65.

In studying these chapters, many have been tempted to concentrate exclusively on the magnificent passages which present his vision of God's universal sovereignty, and then draw a straight contrast between this allegedly 'broadminded' outlook and the 'narrow nationalism' which appears in the writings of the post-exilic age – Haggai, Zechariah, Nehemiah and Ezra.[31] Such a simple universalist message, however, would hardly have raised the drooping spirits of the exiles and that, we must remember, was the prophet's immediate task. In any case, this view cannot survive a fair examination of the evidence. Second Isaiah is, in fact, more passionately concerned with the unique privilege of Israel than any of his predecessors among the independent prophets.[32] It is not for nothing that he borrows from Isaiah of Jerusalem 'the Holy One *of Israel*' as a title for God.[33]

When we drain off the life from the prophet's poetry and compress the residue into a prosaic doctrine of 'monotheism', we miss the whole point of his message. Second Isaiah was not concerned to establish the belief that there was only one God (that, with his predecessors, he took for granted). What he was concerned to do was to convince the despondent exiles that it was *their* God, who had 'measured the waters in the hollow of his hand . . . and weighed the mountains in scales', that it was *their* God, the Holy One of Israel, whose purpose governed all things from the Creation of the world to the coming of Cyrus:

Thus says the LORD, your Redeemer,
   who formed you from the womb:
'I am the LORD, who made all things,
   who stretched out the heavens alone,
   who spread out the earth – Who was with me? –

31. Hag. 2. 10–14; Zech. 1. 18–21; 12. 1–13. 6; 14. 1–21; Neh. 13. 1–3, 23–31; Ezra 4. 1–5; 10. 10–12.
32. Isa. 41. 8–10; 42. 1; 43. 10, 20; 44. 1, 2; 45. 4; 49. 7.
33. Isa. 41. 14, 16, 20; 43. 3; 49. 7.

who frustrates the omens of liars,
   and makes fools of diviners;
who turns wise men back,
   and makes their knowledge foolish;
who confirms the word of his servant,
   and performs the counsel of his messengers;
who says of Jerusalem, "She shall be inhabited,"
   and of the cities of Judah, "They shall be built,
   and I will raise up their ruins;"
who says to the deep, "Be dry,
   I will dry up your rivers;"
who says of Cyrus, "He is my shepherd,
   and he shall fulfil all my purpose;"
saying of Jerusalem, "She shall be built,"
   and of the temple, "Your foundation shall be laid." [34]

The closeness of the relationship between Israel and God, of which all the prophets were convinced, is not lost in the sweep of Second Isaiah's cosmic theology. It is, indeed, the prophet's combination of intimacy and ultimacy which makes his sense of Israel's vocation so strangely moving:

For your Maker is your husband,
   the LORD of hosts is his name;
and the Holy One of Israel is your Redeemer,
   the God of the whole earth he is called.[35]

Theoretically, one might suppose, the special relationship of Israel to God ought to have been forgotten when he was seen to be the God of the whole earth. Second Isaiah, however, was not a theorist, but a prophet; he did not think in doctrinal abstractions, but in terms of history. He was addressing people who believed they had been deserted; his immediate aim was to convince them that they were still the Chosen People and to show them how their destiny was charged with the greatest

34. Isa. 44. 24–8; cf. 51. 12–14.
35. Isa. 54. 5.

possible significance. A choice made by the God of the whole earth was separated by a great gulf from the 'Hobson's Choice' (which was no choice at all) open to the national gods of the surrounding peoples. As a matter of practical and pressing urgency, the danger in which the exiled Jews stood of losing all sense of their vocation had to be matched by an equally powerful grasp of their privilege and responsibility.

Second Isaiah's response to this pastoral problem provided the Hebrew–Christian tradition with one of its most profound concepts – that of the 'Servant of the Lord':

> But you, Israel, my servant,
> Jacob, whom I have chosen,
> the offspring of Abraham, my friend,
> you whom I took from the ends of the earth,
> and called from its farthest corners,
> saying to you, "You are my servant,
> I have chosen you and not cast you off ";
> fear not, for I am with you,
> be not dismayed, for I am your God;
> I will strengthen you, I will help you,
> I will uphold you with my victorious right hand.[36]

Here, plainly, Israel is the Servant whom God has chosen to fulfil his purpose. There are, however, four passages, usually referred to as the 'Servant Songs', in which the term is used of an individual. Among the bewilderingly varied proposals which have been made about the identity of this figure, the suggestion that he is none other than Second Isaiah has much to commend it. His task of affirming God's sovereignty worldwide is presented in the first song (42.1–4) and the prophet himself describes his call and commission not only to Israel but to earth's farthest bounds in the second song (49.1–6):

> The LORD called me from the womb,
> from the body of my mother he named my name.

36. Isa. 41. 8–10; cf. Isa. 44. 1, 2, 21–3; 45. 4.

He made my mouth like a sharp sword,
   in the shadow of his hand he hid me;
he made me a polished arrow,
   in his quiver he hid me away.
And he said to me, 'You are my servant,
   Israel, in whom I will be glorified.'
But I said, 'I have laboured in vain,
   I have spent my strength for nothing and vanity;
yet surely my right is with the LORD,
   and my recompense with my God.'

And now the LORD says,
   who formed me from the womb to be his servant,
to bring Jacob back to him,
   and that Israel might be gathered to him,
   for I am honoured in the eyes of the LORD,
   and my God has become my strength –
he says:
'It is too light a thing that you should be my servant
   to raise up the tribes of Jacob
   and to restore the preserved of Israel;
I will give you as a light to the nations,
   that my salvation may reach to the end of the earth.'[37]

The reminiscences here of the experience of Jeremiah continue even more clearly in the third song (50. 4–9), which depicts the hostility encountered by the prophet.[38] The fourth song (52. 13–53. 12), which, for obvious reasons, has become deeply embedded in Christian tradition, was probably the work of a highly literate man who was converted to discipleship by the prophet's suffering on behalf of his people.

In the personal awareness of its prophetic representative,[39] the magnitude of Israel's responsibility is seen to be commensurate with the magnitude of its privilege. It was called, not for its own salvation only, but to be 'a light to

37. The reference to Israel in v.3 is most probably a later gloss.
38. See Jer. 1. 5, 8–10, 17–19; 11. 18–23; 15. 15–18; 18. 18–23; 20. 7–12.
39. See pp. 50–3.

the nations'. This glorious charge is the answer to the exiles' despair. So far from being lost in the vast emptiness of the world, a people forsaken and without a future, Israel in exile is declared to be the hope of the world, because the world's Creator (to whom their conquerors falsely lay claim) is none other than their own God – the God of Israel.[40] In creating and cherishing Israel,[41] he has made *its* history the key to *all* history. Their coming deliverance through God's conquest of Babylon by Cyrus[42] will be an act of deliverance surpassing even the Exodus in glory[43] and a revelation of the Creator himself to 'the whole world from end to end'.[44] This 'light to the nations' will bring them flocking to acknowledge his lordship in the new Jerusalem.[45] For such a consummation of God's purpose – the purpose underlying and sustaining the whole Creation, the only appropriate language is that of exultant praise:

How beautiful upon the mountains
 are the feet of him who brings good tidings,
who publishes peace, who brings good tidings of good,
 who publishes salvation,
 who says to Zion, 'Your God reigns.'
Hark, your watchmen lift up their voice,
 together they sing for joy;
for eye to eye they see
 the return of the LORD to Zion.
Break forth together into singing,
 you waste places of Jerusalem;
for the LORD has comforted his people,
 he has redeemed Jerusalem.
The LORD has bared his holy arm
 before the eyes of all the nations;

40. Isa. 40. 12–31; 42. 5; 44. 24; 45. 7, 12, 18, 19; 51. 9, 10.
41. Isa. 46. 3, 4.
42. Isa. 44. 24–8; 45. 1–7, 13; 48. 14; cf. 41. 1–5, 25.
43. Isa. 43. 16–20; 52. 11, 12; cf. 48. 20, 21; 49. 9–11; 51. 9–11; 55. 12, 13.
44. Isa. 40. 5; 52. 10.
45. Isa. 45. 14; 49. 7, 14–26; 51. 2–5; cf. 54. 11–17.

and all the ends of the earth shall see
the salvation of our God.[46]

The soaring poetry in which Second Isaiah celebrates God's salvation is kindled, we must never forget, by particular historical expectations. He is making a realistic promise to the exiles about their future history with God, in their own land, after Cyrus had conquered Babylon and Jerusalem had been rebuilt.

EZEKIEL

As our study of Second Isaiah has reminded us, some of the differences between the convictions of the prophets about judgement and salvation are the result of the particular historical situation in which they were called to speak; others arise from the particular theological background and personal experience upon which they drew. The complexity of these factors reduces the significance of any formal comparisons we may attempt to make. It is illuminating, however, to consider the importance each of the prophets attached to *Israel's own response* in relation to its salvation, since this, of course, elucidates their thinking about God himself.

For Amos and Micah, Israel's disobedient indifference to righteousness is completely determinative of its future and Isaiah offers no hope to the people without the response of faith. There can be no doubt that these three thought of God, the righteous Lord of all the nations, as being totally independent of Israel's existence and so it was possible for them to conclude that his repudiation of the people was absolutely final.[47] Hosea, Jeremiah and Second Isaiah seek no less passionately the people's response, but for them, in the final analysis Israel's future depends entirely on the character of God as infallible love. Because God is personally and irrevocably committed to Israel, his own purpose no less than his

46. Isa. 52. 7–10; cf. 42. 10–13; 44. 23; 48. 20, 21; 49. 13; 54. 1–3.
47. See pp. 90–1, 99–101.

people's future is frustrated by its withdrawal from their mutual relationship. A final breach cannot, therefore, be contemplated and so God is presented as taking a new initiative. Through the discipline of judgement, he prepares the way for a fresh start, which, it is promised, will be on a new basis – that of God's enabling grace.[48] It is at this point that their human analogy breaks down, simply because love can only *invite* the response of the beloved; it cannot give that *promise* of attaining the goal to which the prophets were committed by their belief in the invincibility of God's purpose. The tension disclosed here, between thinking of God in terms of a love which cannot coerce and a purpose which cannot be frustrated, is one of the most fundamental paradoxes of theology.

The contribution of Ezekiel to this theological paradox falls emphatically on the recognition of God's invincible purpose. Like Amos, he thinks of God as exercising a sovereign freedom totally independent of Israel's response, but, unlike Amos, he is unable to contemplate its destruction. The salvation of Israel is a necessity, not, however, as for Hosea, because God is bound to his people by love (a relationship he explicitly denies), but because God's own reputation is inextricably tied up with theirs. The basic conviction of the book of Ezekiel affirms that the God of Israel is, and must be seen by the whole world to be, the one and only God: 'I will manifest my holiness among you in the sight of the nations.'[49] He must disclose his deity in and through Israel ('among you'), because he took Israel as his people in the past, although strangely, the purpose of his choice is never adequately explained.[50]

Ezekiel, it is true, presents three long accounts of Israel's history, but all of them are intended to shock the reader by their gross parody of the traditional sacred history.[51] They

48. See pp. 106–8, 113–14, 124–6.
49. Ezek. 20. 41; 28. 25; 36. 23; cf. 38. 16; 39. 27.
50. Ezek. 20. 5; cf. 16. 6–8; 23. 4.
51. Ezek. 16. 1–58; 20. 1–32; 23. 1–35.

represent Israel as having been unspeakably licentious from the very beginning and as having escaped destruction by God, only because his own reputation was inseparable from his people's fortunes: 'But I withheld my hand, and acted *for the sake of my name*, that it should not be profaned in the sight of the nations.'[52] The fall of Jerusalem, like the fall of Samaria,[53] represented an extreme and exceptional case of God's concern for holiness being allowed to triumph over his care for the honour of his name: 'I the LORD have spoken; it shall come to pass, I will do it; I will not go back, I will not spare, I will not repent; according to your ways and your doings I will judge you.'[54]

The 'dirges and laments and words of woe', which Ezekiel is said to have addressed to the exiles in Babylon between 597 and 587 BC,[55] display a fascinating variety of forms and a breadth of curious learning otherwise strange to the prophetic tradition. They present the fall of Jerusalem, however, following the tradition of Amos and Zephaniah,[56] as the Day of the Lord,[57] when the divine wrath was poured out on abominations so monstrous as even to drive God from his sanctuary.[58] Although Ezekiel and his circle were familiar with the moral norms generally accepted by educated men throughout the ancient Near East[59] and, like earlier prophets, condemn the apostasy of political alliances,[60] the weight of the indictment now falls on idolatrous cultic practices. These defile the people's life and outrage God's holiness.[61]

In Ezekiel, God's judgement is not in the least mitigated by any reverence for Israel's sacred tradition. Zion is nothing

---

52. Ezek. 20. 22; cf. 20. 9, 14.
53. Ezek. 23. 1–10.
54. Ezek. 24. 14.
55. Ezek. 2. 9–3. 11.
56. Amos 5. 18–20; Zeph. 1. 7–9, 12–16; 2. 1, 2.
57. Ezek. 7. 10–27; 34. 12; cf. 13. 5; see pp. 18, 82–6.
58. Ezek. 8. 6; cf. 10. 18, 19; 11. 22, 23.
59. Ezek. 9. 9; 11. 1–8; 18. 5–9, 14–17; 22. 27; 34. 4.
60. Ezek. 23. 1–27.
61. Ezek. 8. 1–18; 13. 17, 21; cf. 22. 26; 36. 17.

more than a 'bloody city' of pagan origin[62] and judgement is declared to begin at the house of God.[63] The promise to Abraham provides Israel with no guarantee of security[64] and no righteous remnant is to be spared; the few who manage to escape the sword are to be regarded as witnesses not to God's saving purpose, but to the evident righteousness of his judgement:

> For thus says the Lord GOD: How much more when I send upon Jerusalem my four sore acts of judgement, sword, famine, evil beasts, and pestilence, to cut off from it man and beast! Yet, if there should be left in it any survivors to lead out sons and daughters, when they come forth to you, and you see their ways and their doings, you will be consoled for the evil that I have brought upon Jerusalem, for all that I have brought upon it. They will console you, when you see their ways and their doings; and you shall know that I have not done without cause all that I have done in it, says the Lord GOD.[65]

Although the prophet declares that God has no pleasure in the death of the wicked,[66] he rarely exhorts the people to repent.[67] The formal disputation on responsibility in 18. 1–32, which has been thought to offer the possibility of avoiding judgement by penitence,[68] is probably simply intended to affirm that the exiles are suffering for their own sins and not for those of their parents.[69]

It has been suggested that Ezekiel was a man of great pastoral concern and wished to persuade the exiles to save themselves by wholeheartedly accepting the divine judge-

62. Ezek. 22. 2; 24. 6, 9; 16. 3.
63. Ezek. 7. 22; 9. 6; 24. 21, 25.
64. Ezek. 33. 23–9; cf. Gen. 15. 1–21.
65. Ezek. 14. 21–3; cf. 12. 16; 6. 8–10; 7. 16.
66. Ezek. 18. 21–3.
67. With Ezek. 18. 31, contrast 11. 19 and 36. 26.
68. Cf. Ezek. 3. 16–21; 33. 10–20.
69. Ezek. 18. 1–4; cf. Exod. 34. 7.

ment. If only they acknowledged that they were, indeed, dead in their sins,[70] they would be able to respond to the gracious gift of new life which God was about to make to his people and their land.[71] Although this possibility cannot be denied, in some of the passages promising salvation the response of the people is explicitly excluded and the whole emphasis falls on the necessity of God's action in (so to speak) his own interest:

> It is not for your sake, O house of Israel, that I am about to act, but for the sake of my holy name, which you have profaned among the nations to which you came. And I will vindicate the holiness of my great name . . . and the nations will know that I am the LORD.[72]

So far from Israel's penitence being a condition of salvation, it is presented as its consequence:

> And you shall know that I am the LORD, when I bring you into the land of Israel, the country which I swore to give to your fathers. And there you shall remember your ways and all the doings with which you have polluted yourselves; and you shall loathe yourselves for all the evils that you have committed. And you shall know that I am the LORD, when I deal with you for my name's sake, not according to your evil ways, nor according to your corrupt doings, O house of Israel, says the Lord GOD.[73]

Ezekiel's overriding conviction is that God should be acknowledged by the nations.[74] This was the purpose of Israel's deliverance from Egypt at the Exodus,[75] and it remains the purpose of the coming deliverance of Israel from exile in Babylon:

70. Cf. Ezek. 33. 10, 11.
71. Ezek. 37. 1–14; cf. 34. 11–16, 25–8; 36. 1–15, 16–38; 37. 15–28.
72. Ezek. 36. 22, 23; cf. 36. 32.
73. Ezek. 20. 42–4; cf. 11. 14–21; 16. 59–63; 36. 31, 32.
74. Ezek. 5. 4–8, 14, 15; 20. 14, 22; 32. 10; cf. 25. 7; 26. 6; 39. 7, 21–4.
75. Ezek. 20. 9.

Thus says the Lord GOD: When I gather the house of Israel from the peoples among whom they are scattered, and *manifest my holiness in them in the sight of the nations*, then they shall dwell in their own land which I gave to my servant Jacob. And they shall dwell securely in it, and they shall build houses and plant vineyards. They shall dwell securely, when I execute judgements upon all their neighbours who have treated them with contempt. Then they will know that I am the LORD their God.[76]

The powerfully theocentric (but wholly impersonal and insensitive) doctrine of the book of Ezekiel reflects its unique combination of priestly thinking and prophetic proclamation ('the word of the LORD came to Ezekiel the priest').[77] It illustrates what is likely to happen when a dogmatic way of speaking about God which is accepted as appropriate in the sanctuary is applied more widely to what is actually going on in the world. Ezekiel's convictions about God's holiness and sovereignty over the nations subordinate the complexities of history to the oversimplified assertions characteristic of liturgy. It is fitting, therefore, that the last section of the book should return to the fundamental source of Ezekiel's theology and end with the promise of a new cultus in a new Temple,[78] to which after Israel's judgement the glory of the Lord will return.[79] The assertion of God's invincible sovereignty in history and its reinterpretation in terms of a Temple-centred cultic community give a strongly flavoured foretaste of the developments that were to take place after the Exile.

76. Ezek. 28. 25, 26; cf. 36. 36; 37. 28.
77. Ezek. 1. 3.
78. Ezek. 40–8.
79. Ezek. 43. 1–5.

CHAPTER 8

Salvation in the Restored Community

Israel's salvation for Amos and Micah was a goal beyond hope; for Isaiah of Jerusalem it was no more than a fleeting vision. In the thought of Hosea and Jeremiah, it was the explicit purpose of God's redemptive judgement of his people. During the Exile, Second Isaiah and Ezekiel proclaimed Israel's salvation as a certainty soon to be realized, the former on the grounds of God's infinite greatness, the latter in order that God's infinite greatness should no longer be impugned. Despite such differing views of salvation, these prophets were unanimous in their conviction that Israel fully deserved the judgement that had long been threatened and which was eventually suffered in the Exile. It was left to the men who claimed to be God's spokesmen about 520 BC, when the Jews recently returned from Babylon were struggling to establish a community in Jerusalem, to make light of Israel's responsibility for its captivity. The first of Zechariah's visions betrays this unmistakable change of emphasis:

> Then the angel of the LORD said, 'O LORD of hosts, how long wilt thou have no mercy on Jerusalem and the cities of Judah, against which thou hast had indignation these seventy years?' And the LORD answered gracious and comforting words to the angel who talked with me. So the angel who talked with me said to me, 'Cry out, Thus says the LORD of hosts: I am exceedingly jealous for Jerusalem and for Zion. And I am very angry with the nations that are at ease; *for while I was angry but a little* they furthered the disaster. Therefore, thus says the LORD, I have returned to Jerusalem with compassion; my house shall be built in it, says the LORD of hosts, and the measuring line shall be stretched out over Jerusalem. Cry

again, Thus says the LORD of hosts: My cities shall again overflow with prosperity, and the LORD will again comfort Zion and again choose Jerusalem.'[1]

From the telling admission 'for while I was angry *but a little*', we see how the balance of responsibility for the sufferings of the Exile was gradually being shifted from Israel's own rebellion to the vindictiveness of the nations.[2] It is difficult to think that these gracious and comforting words would have won the approval of the great prophets of the pre-exilic period. Characteristically, they fulfilled their vocation, as Jeremiah admitted, when they 'prophesied war, famine, and pestilence against many countries and great kingdoms'.[3] In the name of God, they challenged an order that was established in apostasy and threatened it with destruction. After the collapse of the kingdom, it was perhaps inevitable that their successors should turn their thoughts to restoration and reconstruction. Men like Zechariah and Haggai were certainly conscious that they were separated by a great gulf from the days of 'the former prophets': 'But now I will not deal with the remnant of this people as in the former days, says the LORD of hosts.'[4]

Zechariah's use of the term 'remnant' here recalls the magnitude of the change that the Exile brought about.[5] Basically, the word 'remnant' means what has been left over after the bulk has been removed – most frequently by violent death or captivity.[6] The contexts in which the Hebrew root is used generally suggest that the residual part is less important than that which has been lost.[7] The prophets before the Exile

---

1. Zech. 1. 12–17.
2. Isa. 10. 5–7; Obad. 10–15; Mic. 7. 7–10; Ezek. 35. 15.
3. Jer. 28. 8.
4. Zech. 8. 11; cf. 1. 4, 5; 7. 7, 12.
5. The following paragraphs are confined to a brief examination of the use of the principal Hebrew verb and related nouns. The general 'idea of the remnant' in such passages as Gen. 7. 23; 18. 23–33; I Kgs. 19. 18; Isa. 1. 9 and Ezek. 11. 19, 20 is not our present concern.
6. Deut. 4. 27; II Kgs. 7. 13; 25. 22; Ezra 1. 4.
7. Exod. 10. 12, 26; Lev. 5. 9; Josh. 11. 22; II Kgs. 24. 14.

most frequently employ the term in its normal, non-technical meaning; as, for example, Jeremiah, who uses it to describe the residue of the people left in Jerusalem after the Babylonian deportation of 597 BC:

> But thus says the LORD: Like the bad figs which are so bad they cannot be eaten, so will I treat Zedekiah the king of Judah, his princes, *the remnant of Jerusalem* who remain in this land, and those who dwell in the land of Egypt. I will make them a horror to all the kingdoms of the earth, to be a reproach, a byword, a taunt, and a curse in all the places where I shall drive them.[8]

Ezekiel, similarly, calls the residue left in Jerusalem a 'remnant', using the term without any special significance or suggestion of hope.[9] But sometimes the pre-exilic prophets deliberately announce that there will be a 'remnant' of the people and then their intention is to give warning of an overwhelming judgement to come. Thus Amos declares:

> For thus says the Lord GOD:
> 'The city that went forth a thousand
>   shall have a hundred *left*,
> and that which went forth a hundred
>   shall have ten *left*
> to the house of Israel.'[10]

The purpose of this dirge is not to promise the preservation of the hundred or the ten, but to threaten the house of Israel with devastating destruction. The threatening suggestion of the term 'remnant' is the most likely explanation of the cryptic name which Isaiah gave to his son:

> And the LORD said to Isaiah, 'Go forth to meet Ahaz, you and Shear-jashub your son, at the end of the conduit of the

8. Jer. 24. 8, 9; cf. 8. 3; 15. 9; 21. 7; 38. 4, 22; 40. 6; 42. 15.
9. Ezek. 5. 10; 6. 12; 9. 8; 11. 13; 17. 21.
10. Amos 5. 3; cf. 3. 12; Exod. 22. 13.

upper pool on the highway to the Fuller's Field, and say to him, "Take heed, be quiet, do not fear, and do not let your heart be faint." '[11]

The name 'Shear-jashub' may mean either 'a remnant will return' or '*only* a remnant will return', as is clear from two later interpretations in the book of Isaiah. In the first passage, the name is read as a promise that a remnant will return to God in penitence[12] and in the second as a message of doom:

For though your people Israel be as the sand of the sea, only a remnant of them will return [*she'ar yāshûbh*]. Destruction is decreed, overflowing with righteousness.[13]

It is probable that Isaiah named his son to convey a warning on some occasion *before* the crisis which faced Judah when he met Ahaz outside the walls of Jerusalem – the child, after all, appears to have been old enough to walk – and that his presence with his father was a reminder of the disaster that would befall, if the king turned to Assyria instead of to God.

After 587 BC, when Jerusalem fell and prophetic threat became historical fact, the exiles (not unnaturally) called themselves the 'remnant'. Such were the pathetically puzzled group who came to Jeremiah, saying:

Let our supplication come before you, and pray to the LORD your God for us, for all this remnant (for we are left but a few of many, as your eyes see us), that the LORD your God may show us the way we should go, and the thing that we should do.[14]

There were those among the exiles, however, who, so far from giving up hope, came to believe that they had been providentially spared. Their confidence found expression in the

11. Isa. 7. 3, 4.
12. Isa. 10. 20, 21.
13. Isa. 10. 22.
14. Jer. 42. 2, 3; cf. 40. 11.

reinterpretation and development of 'remnant' as a technical term.[15] Now it was used to describe their status – no longer as the 'remnant' left over from a divine judgement which had been deserved – but as the Remnant purposed by God for the fulfilment of his covenant promises. The Remnant is the thin red line of loyal faith in a wicked world.

An anonymous oracle now embodied in the book of Micah shows how completely 'remnant' had lost its original threatening significance. It is now associated with a 'strong nation' and contrasted with the limping and damaged residue:

> In that day, says the LORD,
>   I will assemble the lame
> and gather those who have been driven away,
>   and those whom I have afflicted;
> and the lame I will make the *remnant*;
>   and those who were cast off, a strong nation;
> and the LORD will reign over them in Mount Zion
>   from this time forth and for evermore.[16]

It is evident that the so-called 'doctrine of the Remnant', which is often ascribed to Isaiah, arose among the exilic residue.[17] It expressed their confidence that they were still within God's covenanted purpose and would be restored to Jerusalem. There can, of course, be no question of dismissing the assurance of the exilic community as bogus, since assurance is one of the genuine fruits of faith. Nevertheless, religious assurance and complacent optimism are easily confused, and it is hard to avoid the impression that there is a difference in spiritual quality between the hard-won confidence of (say) Second Isaiah and the self-confidence of some of those who boasted that they had been spared as the promised Remnant.

15. Although the term has no explicit doctrinal content in the following passages (all of exilic date), it appears in contexts which express confidence in restoration: Isa. 4. 3; 10. 20, 21; 11. 11, 16; 28. 5, 6; 46. 3, 4; Mic. 2. 12, 13; 7. 18; Zeph. 2. 7, 9; Jer. 23. 3, 4; 31. 7; Zech. 8. 6, 11.
16. Mic. 4. 6, 7; cf. 5. 7, 8; Isa. 37. 32; Jer. 50. 20; Zech. 3. 12, 13; Gen. 45. 7.
17. See p. 98.

HAGGAI AND ZECHARIAH

The books of Haggai and Zechariah (chs. 1–8), from the years 520–518 BC, provide an illuminating introduction to the monumental reinterpretation of prophetic tradition which took place in the restored community after the return from Babylon. Their message is dominated by four major themes.

(1) *Judgement is past and the New Age is dawning.* While the warnings of the pre-exilic prophets are still valid,[18] the disaster they proclaimed now belongs to the past. God has 'returned to Jerusalem with compassion'[19] and Israel stands on the threshold of the promised New Age.[20] The community is about to be purged of all its social evils and of its religious apostasy,[21] so that an idyllic era of peace and prosperity will soon be inaugurated:

> Thus says the LORD of hosts: Old men and old women shall again sit in the streets of Jerusalem, each with staff in hand for very age. And the streets of the city shall be full of boys and girls playing in its streets.[22]

(2) *Salvation is to be appropriated through the life of the Temple.* Haggai centres his whole message on the rebuilding of the Temple and exposes the community's reluctance to engage in the work as demonstrating its careless indifference to God's saving purpose.[23] Zechariah, on the other hand, emphasizes that it is God's return to Jerusalem which makes the rebuilding possible.[24]

(3) *The New Israel is a theocratic community.* Zerubbabel, a grandson of Jehoiachin and, therefore, of the royal house of David, is more to these two prophets than simply the

18. Zech. 1. 1–6; 7. 1–14.
19. Zech. 1. 12–17; 2. 1–5, 10; 8. 1–3, 14–17, 18, 19.
20. Zech. 5. 1–4.
21. Zech. 5. 5–11.
22. Zech. 8. 4, 5; cf. 8. 11–13.
23. Hag. 1. 1–15.
24. Zech. 1. 16; 4. 6–10; 6. 13.

governor of Judah who was appointed by Darius, the Persian. He is no less a person than God's anointed King, worn as his signet ring, to rule the world on his behalf.[25] Zechariah calls him 'the Branch',[26] a term which acquired technical status in contemporary prophecy to describe the promised 'shoot' from the stump of David's family tree.[27] As God's vicegerent, Zerubbabel is represented as ruling the theocratic community in collaboration with Joshua the high priest,[28] the account of whose coronation may have referred originally to that of Zerubbabel as king.[29]

(4) *The inauguration of God's Kingdom heralds the judgement of the nations*. For Haggai, the destruction of the nations is inseparably connected with the accession of Zerubbabel[30] and, as we have seen, Zechariah develops the theme: 'And I am very angry with the nations that are at ease; for while I was angry but a little they furthered the disaster.'[31]

This facile shift of responsibility from Israel to the nations reveals an anxiety about the fact that they still exercise their sovereignty undisturbed and it is to this concern that the prophet returns in his 'visions':

And I lifted my eyes and saw, and behold, four horns! And I said to the angel who talked with me, 'What are these?' And he answered me, 'These are the horns which have scattered Judah, Israel, and Jerusalem.' Then the LORD showed me four smiths. And I said, 'What are these coming to do?' He answered, 'These are the horns which scattered Judah, so that no man raised his head; and these have come to terrify them, to cast down the horns of the nations who lifted up their horns against the land of Judah to scatter it.'[32]

25. Hag. 2. 23; cf. Jer. 22. 24.
26. Zech. 3. 8; 6. 12.
27. Isa. 11. 1; Jer. 23. 5, 6; 33. 14–16.
28. Zech. 6. 13; cf. 4. 14; Jer. 33. 17–22.
29. Zech. 6. 9–14.
30. Hag. 2. 20–3.
31. Zech. 1. 15.
32. Zech. 1. 18–21; see also 6. 1–8.

These 'visions' make it clear that he recognizes the community's desire to be avenged of its former oppressors and to be reassured about the reality of God's universal dominion.[33] He therefore promises that the nations will be reduced to subservience,[34] or else destroyed.[35]

ANONYMOUS PROPHECY

The four themes of Haggai and Zechariah are reflected so often in the large volume of anonymous salvation oracles now scattered throughout the prophetic literature that they also may be taken to represent the work of men who were engaged in reinterpreting the tradition at about the same time.

(1) *Judgement is past and the New Age is dawning.* The most sustained and eloquent announcement of God's intention to reverse his people's fortunes comes from the anonymous prophet who continued the work of Second Isaiah:

> For I will not contend for ever,
>   nor will I always be angry;
> for from me proceeds the spirit,
>   and I have made the breath of life.
> Because of the iniquity of his covetousness
>   I was angry,
> I smote him, I hid my face and was angry;
> but he went on backsliding in the way of
>   his own heart.
> I have seen his ways, but I will heal him;
>   I will lead him and requite him with comfort.[36]

The nations, he declares, will come streaming in with their tribute to the New Jerusalem,[37] over whom God rejoices as a

33. Zech. 2. 8, 9.
34. Zech. 8. 20–3.
35. Zech. 1. 21; 6. 7.
36. Isa. 57. 16–18; cf. 60. 1–18, 21, 22; 61. 1–11; 62. 1–12; 65. 17–25; 66. 6–14.
37. Isa. 60. 1–18.

bridegroom over his bride.[38] Divine wrath, desertion, devastation, desolation, premature death, jeers, insults – are now all left behind; the future before Israel holds nothing but the joy of salvation. Other oracles in the secondary tradition of the book of Isaiah repeat these motifs – the peaceful ingathering of the nations[39] and the unprecedented prosperity and tranquillity of the New Age,[40] when 'sorrow and sighing shall flee away'.[41]

(2)   *Salvation is to be appropriated through the life of the Temple.* Prophecy had now returned to the security of its original home in the sanctuary.[42] It had demanded the insight and courage of a Second Isaiah to take the promises which had been confidently made in the worship of the Temple (where, of course, they were not exposed to falsification by the facts of life) and relate them to the realities of Israel's historical situation in exile.[43] He did so, moreover, in the full knowledge that the limitless claims of their liturgical language were doomed to non-fulfilment. By contrast, Haggai and Zechariah made promises about the restoration of the Temple, which they expected would be fulfilled quite literally. For Second Isaiah, as for his anonymous disciple, the rebuilding of the Temple was merely a subsidiary consequence of Israel's historical deliverance,[44] but for Ezekiel and his successors, it was the consummation of the people's return and the means of their salvation.[45] Under their influence, the whole prophetic tradition came to be annexed by the Jerusalem community and built into the foundations of post-exilic Judaism.

The close association of prophecy with the Temple about the year 350 BC is admirably illustrated by the work of the Chronicler. He constantly claims to know sources attributed

38. Isa. 62. 1–12.
39. Isa. 2. 2–4; cf. Mic. 4. 1–4.
40. Isa. 32. 15–20; 33. 20–4; cf. Amos 9. 13–15.
41. Isa. 35. 1–10; cf. Jer. 29. 10–14; 31. 10–14; 32. 36–44; 33. 6–11.
42. See pp. 32–5.
43. See pp. 124–6.
44. Isa. 44. 28; 60. 7, 13; cf. 56. 3–8; 66. 20, 21.
45. Ezek. 40–8.

to prophets,[46] and prophets are often introduced into his narrative to provide edifying discourses.[47] These sermons almost certainly reflect the style of religious instruction given by the Temple Levites as they 'went round the towns of Judah teaching the people'[48] and it is interesting to observe that it was based on the prophets as well as the Law: 'Hear me, Judah and inhabitants of Jerusalem! *Believe* in the Lord your God, and *you will be established*; believe his prophets, and you will succeed.'[49] The Levites who in this way reinterpreted the teaching of the prophets for their own time are clearly regarded by the Chronicler as their true successors. That is why he substitutes 'Levites' for 'prophets' in the account of Josiah's reform which he found in his source[50] and describes the function of the Levitical singers as 'prophesying'.[51] It was, we may note, the view of later rabbinic tradition that the spirit of prophecy had passed to the scribes.[52] After the Exile, the prophetic tradition as a whole, it seems, was reinterpreted as a promise of salvation after judgement and the theocratic community, as represented by the Chronicler, could claim that in the blessings of its Temple-centred life this prophetic promise had found its final fulfilment.[53]

(3) *The New Israel is a theocratic community.* According to the royal theology of the pre-exilic Temple, Israel was not a kingdom in the political sense but a theocratic community. It was God who reigned as its King[54] and David and his dynastic successors ruled as his vicegerent.[55] His inviolable covenant with the house of David[56] came to be regarded as the firmest

46. I Chron. 29. 29; II Chron. 9. 29; 12. 15; 13. 22; 20. 34; 21. 12; 32. 32; 33. 19.
47. II Chron. 12. 5–8; 15. 1–7; 16. 7–10; 19. 2, 3; 20. 13–18, 37; 28. 9–11.
48. II Chron. 17. 7–9 (REB); 35. 3; cf. 30. 6–10; Neh. 8. 7, 8.
49. II Chron. 20. 20; cf. Isa. 7. 9.
50. II Chron. 34. 30; cf. II Kgs. 23. 2.
51. I Chron. 25. 1–6; II Chron. 20. 1–30.
52. Cf. II Chron. 29. 25; see p. 148.
53. Cf. II Chron. 36. 20–3; see p. 155.
54. Ps. 47; 93; 96; 97; 98; 99; cf. Ps. 5. 2; 24. 7–10.
55. Ps. 2. 7–9; 110. 1, 5–7.
56. II Sam. 7. 4–17; Ps. 89. 19–37.

guarantee of the nation's security.[57] That this confidence was not entirely shattered by the fall of Jerusalem is evident from a number of anonymous oracles, now embodied in the prophetic literature alongside other exilic oracles of salvation, which promise that the throne of David will be re-established.[58] It is even possible that the deuteronomic teachers, pinning their hopes on the exiled Jehoiachin,[59] shared this expectation and are responsible for its place in the secondary tradition of the book of Jeremiah.[60] Despite the explicit interest of the secondary tradition of the book of Isaiah in the Davidic monarchy and its restoration,[61] Second Isaiah actually denies all such expectations by transferring the promise of the Davidic covenant from the king to the people as a whole:

Ho, every one who thirsts, come to the waters;
   and he who has no money,
     come, buy and eat!
Come, buy wine and milk
   without money and without price.
Why do you spend your money for that which is not bread,
   and your labour for that which does not satisfy?
Hearken diligently to me, and eat what is good,
   and delight yourselves in fatness.
Incline your ear, and come to me;
   hear, that your soul may live;
and I will make with you an everlasting covenant,
   my steadfast, sure love for David.[62]

The Davidic hope is also no more than marginal in the tradition of Ezekiel,[63] where the 'prince', as he is called, is

57. See pp. 96–8, 137–8.
58. Amos 9. 11, 12; Hos. 3.5; Mic. 5. 2–4; Zech. 9. 9, 10; 12. 7–10; cf. Hos. 1. 10–2.1.
59. II Kgs. 25. 27–30; cf. Jer. 28. 4.
60. Jer. 17. 24, 25; 23. 3–8; 30. 8, 9; 33. 14–16, 17–26.
61. Isa. 9. 2–7; 11. 1–9, 10; cf. 32. 1–8.
62. Isa. 55. 1–3.
63. Ezek. 34. 23, 24; 37. 24, 25; cf. 17. 22–4.

firmly subordinated to the priestly theocracy of the Temple community.[64]

It is misleading to represent this hope of the restoration of David's line as 'Messianism', since it differs significantly from that expectation of a political Messianic Deliverer, which arose at the end of the Old Testament period and is to be found, for example, in the Psalms of Solomon:

> Behold, O Lord, and raise up unto them their king, the son
>   of David,
>   At the time in the which Thou seest, O God,
>   that he may reign over Israel Thy servant.
> And gird him with strength, that he may shatter unrighteous
> rulers,
> And that he may purge Jerusalem from nations that trample
>   [her] down to destruction.[65]

In the Old Testament, it is always God's Kingdom which brings the 'Messiah',[66] and not the Messiah who brings in the Kingdom. In the post-exilic community, the Davidic hope was short-lived and relatively insignificant, largely because the priestly theocracy rapidly absorbed the remnants of the old royal theology. To judge by the evidence of the Chronicler, the figure of David became totally detached from history and symbolized little more than the divine favour which the true Israel enjoyed in the Temple and its worship.

(4) *The inauguration of God's Kingdom heralds the judgement of the nations.* The affirmation of God's sovereignty over all the nations had been a major feature of Temple worship and of the institutional prophecy which was so closely associated with it from the establishment of the monarchy.[67] The continuing influence of the institutional

---

64. Ezek. 45. 17; 45. 22–46. 18.
65. Psalms of Solomon, 17. 23, 24 (translation by G.B. Gray, in *The Apocrypha and Pseudepigrapha*, ed. R.H. Charles, vol. II).
66. Cf. Isa. 52. 7; Mic. 4. 7; 5. 2–4; Zeph. 3. 14, 15.
67. See pp. 34–5, 130–1.

prophets during the exilic period and the early years of the restoration is remarkable after the traumatic loss of the Temple and every vestige of national sovereignty. Nevertheless, it may be clearly seen in the large volume of oracles against foreign nations that circulated among the Babylonian exiles before being collected into the blocks now to be found in the middle of each of the major prophetic books.[68]

One of the strangest features of these collections against foreign nations is their inclusion of anonymous oracles on Israel's smaller neighbours: Damascus,[69] the Philistines,[70] Tyre,[71] Edom,[72] Ammon,[73] and Moab.[74] While it seems possible to account for the oracles against Edom by reference to its overt hostility to the Jews after the fall of Jerusalem,[75] there is no reliable evidence that the other small nations did anything particularly to deserve the prophets' wrath at this period. How, then, did this consensus about their fate arise? It is tempting to speculate that the explanation lies in a well-established ritual practice among the cultic prophets of the pre-exilic period. A regular catalogue of foreign peoples, we may suppose, became current, which listed 'all the nations' and therefore symbolized the concept of God's universal sovereignty.[76]

This possibility is strengthened by the fact that all six nations find a place in the series of reproaches with which the book of Amos begins.[77] With the exception of the oracles against Tyre[78] and Edom,[79] which may have been added after the fall of Jerusalem, this tally of nations comes from the eighth cen-

68. Isa. 13–23; Jer. 25. 15–38; with 46–51; Ezek. 25–32; see p. 155.
69. Jer. 49. 23–7.
70. Jer. 47. 1–7; Ezek. 25. 15–17.
71. Isa. 23. 1–18; Ezek. 26. 1–28. 19; cf. Jer. 47.4.
72. Isa. 34. 1–17; Jer. 49. 7–22.
73. Jer. 49. 1–6; Ezek. 25. 1–7.
74. Isa. 15. 1–9; 16. 6–12; Jer. 48. 1–47; Ezek. 25. 8–11.
75. Ps. 137. 7; Lam. 4. 21, 22; Mal. 1. 2–5; Obad. 1–18.
76. Cf. Num. 24. 15–19; Ps. 60. 8; 83. 6–8; Jer. 25. 15–29.
77. Amos 1. 3–2. 16.
78. Amos 1. 9, 10.
79. Amos 1. 11, 12.

tury BC. It is, of course, obvious that the oracles of Amos differ considerably in style, content and purpose from the institutional prophets' oracles against the nations. They are brief, specific in their accusations, explicitly moral in their point of view and, so far from promising salvation to Israel, are clearly intended to establish God's universal sovereignty as a setting for Amos' proclamation that Israel would not escape the nations' fate. Despite these differences, it is probable that Amos had exploited a traditional pattern of denunciation. This would explain his repeated formula, 'I will send a fire upon . . . and it shall devour',[80] as deriving from the conventional language used by the institutional prophets in proclaiming Holy War.[81] In the anonymous oracles against the nations written after the fall of Jerusalem, it was the original intention of these denunciations which was stridently reasserted:

Therefore all who devour you shall be devoured,
    and all your foes, every one of them, shall go into captivity;
those who despoil you shall become a spoil,
    and all who prey on you I will make a prey.[82]

It is significant that many of these oracles present Israel's triumph over its enemies as the Day of the Lord, completely indifferent to the fact that the great independent prophets, like Amos, had turned its meaning upside down.[83]

There were, however, a few exceptions. Some of these anonymous prophets held out a promise that the nations would come to acknowledge God's sovereignty and so escape destruction.[84] It was, however, only a tiny minority who had the vision to interpret this sovereignty as eliciting the Gentiles' *willing* response.[85]

80. Amos 1. 4, 7, 14; 2. 2.
81. Jer. 49. 27; 50. 32; cf. Hos. 8. 14; Jer. 17. 27; 21. 14; see pp. 85–6.
82. Jer. 30. 16; cf. Mic. 4. 11–13; Isa. 60. 12; Isa. 49. 22–6; Deut. 30. 7.
83. Isa. 13. 6, 9; 34. 8; Jer. 46. 10; Ezek. 30. 3; Joel 3. 14; Obad. 15; Zech. 14. 1; cf. Ezek. 38–9; see pp. 82–3.
84. Isa. 14. 1, 2; 60. 1–22; 66. 18–23; Zeph. 2. 10, 11; Zech. 14. 16–19.
85. Isa. 56. 1–8; Zeph. 3. 9; cf. Isa. 19. 19–22, 23–5.

There were other minorities. Not all the members of the post-exilic community took the view that it constituted a theocracy in which all God's promises and purposes had already been fulfilled. From time to time, dissident groups spoke out and declared that Jerusalem was far from being the perfect embodiment of the Kingdom of God. The book Malachi, for example, provides significant evidence of disappointment and disillusionment only half a century after the rebuilding of the Temple. It exposes a high degree of scepticism in the community,[86] slovenly indifference in the priesthood[87] and disintegration in society at large.[88] It was in opposition to this decline that groups of Jews deliberately separated themselves from the common herd and, on the basis of the prophetic teaching they had inherited, cultivated the expectation of a coming judgement, in which they (the righteous) would be distinguished from the wicked and at last vindicated:

> Then those who feared the LORD spoke with one another; the LORD heeded and heard them, and a book of remembrance was written before him of those who feared the LORD and thought on his name. They shall be mine, says the LORD of hosts, my special possession on the day when I act, and I will spare them as a man spares his son who serves him. Then once more you shall distinguish between the righteous and the wicked, between one who serves God and one who does not serve him.[89]

As is illustrated by this passage from Malachi, the God-fearers left their mark on the prophetic tradition by reinterpreting a number of its key oracles, so that their threats of judgement were made to apply to the faithless majority in the Jewish community, and the promises of salvation to their own eclectic group.[90] Further examples of such reinterpretation may be found in Joel, where the promise of the

86. Mal. 1.2; 2. 17–3.5; 3. 13–15.
87. Mal. 1.6–2.9.
88. Mal. 2.10–16; cf. Mic. 7.1–6.
89. Mal. 3. 16–18; cf. Zeph. 2.3; 3.11–13.
90. Isa. 57.1, 2, 13, 21; 65. 8–16; 66. 1–5.

Spirit appears to have been annexed by a minority who, it is said, 'call upon the name of the LORD',[91] and, similarly, in Zechariah, where the preservation of a purified remnant is envisaged:

> In the whole land, says the LORD,
>   two thirds shall be cut off and perish,
>   and one third shall be left alive.
> And I will put this third into the fire,
>   and refine them as one refines silver,
>   and test them as gold is tested.
> They will call on my name,
>   and I will answer them.
> I will say, 'They are my people';
>   and they will say, 'The LORD is my God.'[92]

It is probable that the late and extremely obscure collection of prophetic-type material on the Final Judgement in Isaiah, chapters 24–7 also originated in one of these dissident groups. Its members were evidently bold enough to reject the current orthodoxy that God's salvation was already realized in the contemporary theocratic community of Jerusalem. When, as was inevitable, their heretical views involved them in conflict with their fellow Jews, they sought consolation in the hope that in the end they – the Elect – would be vindicated.[93]

91. Joel 2. 28, 29, 32.
92. Zech. 13. 8, 9.
93. Isa. 26. 20, 21; cf. Isa. 2. 10–11.

CHAPTER 9

The Scripture of the Prophets

FROM ORACLES TO BOOKS

In post-exilic Israel – certainly after the time of Ezra (400 BC) – prophecy was encountered not as a living institution, but as a body of authoritative scripture received from the past. No doubt charismatic individuals emerged from time to time and made an impact on the community, but it is improbable that they thought of themselves or were considered by others as direct successors to men like Amos, Isaiah and Jeremiah. These were the great 'former prophets', whose teaching was now treasured in written form.[1] It was commonly held that the old kind of prophecy ended with Malachi – a view expressed in a famous rabbinic statement: 'When the last prophets, Haggai, Zechariah and Malachi died, the holy spirit ceased in Israel.' The same understanding is illustrated by references to the absence of a prophet during the Maccabean crisis (167–164 BC): 'It was a time of harsh oppression for Israel, worse than any since the days when prophets ceased to appear among them.'[2]

The growth and interpretation of prophetic scripture in the post-exilic age are shrouded in obscurity. As the literary criticism of the books as we now have them so clearly demonstrates,[3] it is impossible to trace the lines of development with any precision. One of the few certain facts is that the corpus had attained its present form by about 190 BC, when Jesus ben Sira, in his book Ecclesiasticus, gave a brief survey of the four great collections of prophetic oracles: Isaiah (Ecclus. 48. 17–25), Jeremiah (Ecclus. 49. 1–7), Ezekiel

1. Zech. 1. 1–6; 7. 7, 12.
2. I Macc. 9. 27 (REB); 4. 44–7; 14. 41.
3. See pp. 12–28.

(Ecclus. 49. 8, 9) and the twelve minor prophets (Ecclus. 49. 10). These 'books' bear witness to the convictions and concerns of the post-exilic community, for it was only then that they were fashioned into their final shape. The main aim of historical scholarship has been to identify in this mass of material those parts of it which bear reliable witness to the convictions and concerns of the prophets themselves.

The independent prophets were primarily public speakers, who characteristically communicated their teaching in brief poetic oracles, introduced for the most part by a formula of the kind used by messengers throughout the ancient Near East – 'Thus says the LORD'.[4] The unexpected and shocking content of the prophets' message was matched by their unexpected and shocking exploitation of all sorts of familiar forms and styles. Thus we find, for example, prophetic versions of the priestly direction,[5] the funeral dirge,[6] the liturgical lament,[7] the legal indictment,[8] the trial scene,[9] the disputation,[10] the school lesson,[11] and even the popular song.[12] The very daring of the prophets' way of getting their message across illustrates their freedom and confirms their independent status as laymen. The fact that it is a *finished* style raises a number of complicated questions many of which cannot be answered with any degree of confidence.

Did Amos, the first known practitioner of this finished style, create it himself, or did he inherit it? If he inherited it, from whom and through which channels did it reach him? Although, according to our records, Amos is the first prophet of his particular kind, it is always possible that there were comparable prophets earlier, who either have disappeared

---

4. Cf. Gen. 32. 3–5; Ezra 1. 2; I Kgs. 2. 30.
5. Isa. 1. 10–17.
6. Amos 5. 2.
7. Hos. 6. 1–3.
8. Isa. 3. 13–15.
9. Isa 41. 1–5, 21–9; 43. 8–13; 45. 20–5.
10. Isa. 40. 12–17, 18–26, 27–31.
11. Amos 3. 1–8.
12. Isa. 5. 1–7; 22. 13; see p. 96.

without trace, or now appear in the biblical record in a form which misrepresents their true character. Elijah (from about 850 BC) is the most obvious example of a prophetic figure who may well have resembled Amos much more closely than is suggested by the popular biographical narratives in which the memory of him has been preserved.[13] This possibility further suggests that what we know as 'written' prophecy may have emerged in the eighth century BC simply because it was only then that the independent kind of prophet made contact with educated scribes from a school tradition capable of preserving and transmitting his teaching. The opportunity for speculation is endless. However, whether or not Amos was the first of the independent prophets and whether or not he himself created the prophetic style, his skilled use of it and the faithful preservation of his oracles both point to an association with a stable educational institution.

The question of how the prophets' oracles came to be preserved gains in significance when we see that it has a direct bearing on the question of what kind of people they themselves were. That is to say, a man is known by the company he keeps. Some scholars take the view that for the preservation of the prophets' oracles we are primarily indebted to their own intimate circles of disciples. It is held that the disciples learnt by heart the content of their master's teaching and transmitted it to their successors by word of mouth, until finally, perhaps as late as the period of the Exile, it was recorded in writing. Other scholars hold a modified version of this theory and assert that the oracles were handed down partly in written and partly in oral form, with mutual interaction between the two. Such a hypothesis is possible, but serious problems remain.

If the independent prophets were laymen and if, as seems probable, their so-called ministries were not lifelong commissions but occasional and brief interventions in the affairs of their community, it is very difficult to believe that they surrounded themselves with circles of disciples. The ministry of

13. I Kgs. 17. 1–24; 18. 20–40; 19. 1–18; 21. 1–20; II Kgs. 2. 1–8; see pp. 39–41.

Jeremiah is exceptional in that it seems to have been permanent, but even he is never seen in the company of any circle of disciples.[14] Elisha is the one case of a prophet who is known to have cultivated disciples, but the kind of wonder-working tradition they transmitted about their master does not provide a very promising model for understanding the practice of later prophets.[15] Even if it were conceivable that men like Amos and Micah attracted disciples in their lifetime, it is impossible to suppose that small circles of devotees remained in being, generation after generation, solely to treasure and transmit orally a small amount of the master's teaching, until, two centuries later, they relinquished their task to a sympathetic scribe. The preservation of the prophets' teaching demands a transmitting agency of much greater stability than anything they themselves could possibly have created.

What that transmitting agency may have been is suggested by the only detailed evidence we possess about the recording of spoken oracles and this occurs in the book of Jeremiah.[16] Two features of Jeremiah's situation are significant. First, he had a secretary to whom he dictated his oracles; second, he was in close touch with a family of educated and influential citizens, who showed their sympathy with his teaching by protecting him on more than one occasion when he fell foul of the authorities. It is at least possible that this group demonstrated their sympathy with the prophet in a more permanent way by helping to preserve his collected oracles.[17] Although, no doubt, Jeremiah's circumstances were in some ways unrepresentative, there is no reason why the independent prophets of the eighth century should not equally have enjoyed the support of some of their contemporaries and, again, no reason why these sympathizers should not have been sufficiently educated to preserve the prophets' oracles in writing.

14. See pp. 108–14.
15. II Kgs. 2. 1–18.
16. Jer. 36. 1–32; see pp. 25–7.
17. Jer. 26. 1–19, 24.

Literacy in ancient Israel was more widespread than is often supposed,[18] the pre-exilic prophets were certainly acquainted with the teaching of the schools,[19] and there are explicit references to the prophets writing down their own oracles.[20] This suggests an explanation for the crispness with which the prophets' oracles have been preserved; it points to the schools and their libraries as an established and stable method of transmission,[21] which no private circles of disciples could possibly have provided; and it helps explain the common features and continuity between the individual prophets.[22] Since the school tradition was far from monochrome, it is not surprising that a variety of scribal styles have been detected, such as the deuteronomic in the book of Jeremiah,[23] the priestly in Ezekiel[24] and that of the circle of teachers who produced the books of Chronicles in Haggai and Zechariah.

EDITING AND INTERPRETATION

The fact that it is possible to identify the work of different scribes in the prophetic books confirms the evidence that, so far from being mere copyists, they were the men responsible for interpreting the scriptures – editing, amplifying and structuring the texts to bring out their meaning for their own times. Their approach was determined not only by their contemporary concerns, but also, and more fundamentally, by their conviction that in them were embodied God-given truths and mysteries otherwise unavailable. Although the evidence does not enable us to plot in detail how this work of interpretation developed and helped shape the written

18. Isa. 29. 11, 12; Ezek. 37. 15–20; Jer. 51. 60; Job 31. 35–6.
19. Amos 3. 3–8; 6. 12; cf. Prov. 6. 27. 28; Isa. 10. 15; 29. 15–16; cf. Jer. 18. 1–6, 13–16; see pp. 61–3.
20. Isa. 8. 1–4; 30. 8; Hab. 2. 2; Jer. 30. 2.
21. II Macc. 2. 13, 14; cf. II Chron. 35. 25.
22. See p. 14.
23. See p. 23.
24. See p. 131.

tradition during the first three centuries of the post-exilic age, it is at least possible to identify two main objectives – the discovery in the scriptures of moral guidance and their contribution to theological reflection on the vexed subject of God's providential rule. To these two approaches may be added the late and eccentric apocalyptic development, which was cultivated by sects living in the expectation that the world was about to end.[25]

Of these dominant types of interpretation, the least unexpected is that which found moral guidance in the prophetic tradition to amplify and illustrate the all-authoritative Law of Moses. From the end of the post-exilic age, we even have a statement which goes so far as to claim that the teaching of Jeremiah was actually based on the Law: 'After giving them the law, the prophet charged them not to neglect the ordinances of the Lord, or let their minds be led astray by the sight of the gold and silver images in all their finery.'[26] From the same period, the attractive book of Tobit confirms the strong contribution of prophetic teaching to the accepted moral tradition of the community: 'Keep the Lord in mind every day of your life, my son, and never deliberately do what is wrong or violate his commandments . . . Pay any man who works for you his wages that same day; let no one wait for his money . . . Do to no one what you yourself would hate. Do not drink to excess or let drunkenness become a habit. Share your food with the hungry, your clothes with those who have none.'[27]

The second main aim in the interpretation of the prophetic scriptures was to uncover reassuring theological affirmations, especially about God's control of history and his final goal for the world. It was principally intended to establish that, despite all evidence to the contrary, God could be trusted, as the final verses of Habakkuk splendidly declare:

25. See pp. 157–62.
26. II Macc. 2.2 (REB).
27. Tobit 4. 5, 14–16 (REB); cf. Jer. 22. 13–17; Isa. 1. 16; 5. 11–13, 22–3; 28. 1–8; Amos 4. 1, 2.

> Though the fig tree do not blossom,
>   nor fruit be on the vines,
> the produce of the olive fail,
>   and the fields yield no food,
> the flock be cut off from the fold
>   and there be no herd in the stalls.
> Yet I will rejoice in the LORD;
>   I will joy in the God of my salvation.[28]

Another application of this confidence is found in the book of Tobit, where the author (writing about 200 BC but presented as living in the eighth century BC and as interpreting prophecy as authoritative prediction), presents a 'forecast' of Israel's history as being very firmly under God's direction:

'When he was dying, [Tobit] sent for his son Tobias and gave him these instructions: "My son, you must take your children and be off to Media with all haste, for I believe God's word spoken against Nineveh by Nahum. It will all come true; everything will happen to Asshur and Nineveh that was spoken by the prophets of Israel who were sent by God. Not a word of it will fall short; all will take place in due time . . . I know, I am convinced, that all God's words will be fulfilled . . . Our countrymen who live in Israel will all be scattered and carried off into captivity . . . But God will have mercy on them again and bring them back to the land of Israel . . . Then they will . . . rebuild Jerusalem in splendour; then indeed God's house will be built in her as the prophets of Israel foretold. All the nations in the whole world will be converted to the true worship of God . . . and will praise the eternal God in righteousness." '[29]

There is no suggestion here that the author of Tobit thought of the consummation of God's purpose as being imminent;

---

28. Hab. 3. 17, 18.
29. Tobit 14. 3–7 (REB).

the point is simply that the faithful may rest assured that in the end all will be well.

The same teaching probably accounts for the structure the editors imposed on the three books of the major prophets. Each is arranged in a three-fold pattern: (*a*) *oracles on the judgement of Israel* (Isa. 1–12; Jer. 1.1–25.14; Ezek. 1–24); (*b*) *oracles on the judgement of the nations* (Isa. 13–23; Jer. 25. 15–38, followed immediately, as in the Septuagint (Greek) version, by 46–51; Ezek. 25–32); (*c*) *oracles on the salvation of Israel* (Isa. 24–66; Jer. 26–35; Ezek. 33–48). It is reasonable to suppose that the pattern of these books was established in two stages and that each reflects a distinct attempt at theological interpretation. The first stage brought together (*a*) and (*b*) to produce a two-part 'judgement–salvation' pattern, such as may be found on a small scale in the book of Micah, where the proclamation of judgement (chs. 1–3) is followed by the promise of salvation (chs. 4–5). This pattern, it is suggested, represents the earliest and simplest theological position adopted in the post-exilic community: it is affirming that God had brought the time of judgement to an end and had now re-established the fortunes of his people.[30] In the second stage of the development this pattern was elaborated to produce the final three-part scheme by the interpolation of (*b*) – oracles on the judgement of the nations. How may this addition be explained? It is impossible to be confident, but it seems to be connected with the anxious awareness of the post-exilic community that God's work of salvation for Israel was lamentably incomplete. Despite all the oracles of doom on the nations, they continued to prosper with undiminished vigour and so it is not surprising that these unfulfilled predictions presented an awkward problem for the faithful. The editors' way of dealing with it was to detach the oracles from any expectation of *imminent* fulfilment and represent them as simply marking a stage in God's predetermined and orderly plan.

It is not difficult to detect the intellectual background of this kind of interpretation. Discerning *orderly patterns* in the

30. Cf. Isa. 40. 1, 2; 54. 7, 8; Jer. 32. 42; see pp. 137–43.

chaos of experience was a basic preoccupation of Israel's scribes, as it had been for two thousand years among the learned men of Babylon and Egypt. Later, the Greek philosophers engaged in a comparable kind of analysis, as we find it reflected in the book Ecclesiasticus:

> Look at all the works of the Most High –
> they are in pairs, one the counterpart of the other.
> His works endure, all of them active for ever
> and all responsive to their several functions.[31]

Similarly, the scribes analysed Israel's history and *divided it into periods*, as in the editing of the narratives presenting the pre-exilic age and, most explicitly, in the book of Daniel.[32] However, whereas in Daniel the scheme of the successive world-empires was exploited to identify the time of the end – the *imminent* consummation of history, elsewhere the division of history into periods was fundamentally an assertion about providence – a way of declaring that whatever present experience suggested, it was, nevertheless, part of the pattern of God's sovereign purpose for his people. It seems probable that the alternation of judgement and blessing in many of the prophetic books was designed to convey the same teaching. Belief in divine order, which is at the heart of the scribal interpretation of the scriptures, is most memorably expressed in the book of Judith: 'All that happened then, and all that happened before and after, was your work. What is now and what is yet to be, you have planned; and what you have planned has come to pass.'[33]

31. Ecclus. 33. 15; 42. 23 (REB).
32. Dan. 2. 31–45; 7. 1–27; 9. 20–7.
33. Judith 9. 5 (REB).

CHAPTER 10

Prophetic Foreknowledge of the Imminent End

During the period 300 BC to AD 300 a new kind of writing emerged and flourished in Judaea; it is generally known as 'apocalyptic' (from the Greek meaning 'to uncover'), because it claimed to reveal secrets. The revelations are represented as having been made to an ancient seer or sage, character- istically, but not invariably, in visions.[1] Their content covers a wide range of esoteric subjects – cosmology, astronomy, meteorology, mythology, the celestial world, the underworld *and the end of the world*. Not all apocalypses include revela- tions about the end of the world, but those that do, represent it not as an event in the remote future but as the *imminent* and final act of God for the consummation of his purpose.

The only apocalypse to gain admission to the Hebrew scriptures is the book of Daniel, written in the name of a legendary hero of the Exile to meet the tremendous crisis of 167–164 BC, when the Greek king, Antiochus IV Epiphanes, defiled the Temple and proscribed the practice of the Jewish religion. The most curious feature of the work, especially in view of the perilous situation and the urgent demands it made for the direct encouragement of the faithful to endure, is the tortuous and obscurely learned way in which it presents its relatively simple message.

The writer, or writers,[2] must be reckoned as belonging to

---

1. As, for example, in The Book of Enoch, The Apocalypse of Abraham, The Assumption of Moses and The Testament of Job.
2. The book is almost certainly the work of at least two authors. The stories of chs. 1–6 were drawn from a wider literature about the hero Daniel and probably date from the third century BC; the visions of chs. 7–12 were written for the crisis in the second century.

the select group of teachers who are referred to as 'the wise'[3] and who evidently had at their command a considerable knowledge of history,[4] mythology,[5] and (above all) the scriptures.[6] The obscurity of their exposition is largely attributable to the method they employ in interpreting the scriptures and other God-given 'revelations'. A text of Jeremiah, for example, which refers to an exile of seventy years, is interpreted by the angel Gabriel to mean a period of 490 years, so that it neatly predicts the crisis of 167–164 BC:

> I, Daniel, was reading the scriptures and reflecting on the seventy years which, according to the word of the LORD to the prophet Jeremiah, were to pass while Jerusalem lay in ruins. Then I turned to the Lord God in earnest prayer and supplication with fasting and with sackcloth and ashes ... I was still praying, when the man Gabriel, whom I had already seen in the vision, flew close to me at the hour of the evening offering. He explained to me: 'Daniel, I have now come to enlighten your understanding ... Consider well the word, consider the vision: seventy times seven years are marked out for your people and your holy city; then rebellion will be stopped, sin brought to an end, iniquity expiated, everlasting right ushered in, vision and prophecy ratified, and the Most Holy Place anointed.'[7]

Similarly, royal dreams and a cryptic inscription are represented as 'mysteries',[8] of which the meaning may be known only through an authoritative 'interpretation'.[9] It is for the task of interpretation that Daniel is said to have been divinely endowed with 'wisdom'.[10]

3. Dan. 12. 3; 11. 33, 35; cf. 12. 10.
4. Dan. 2. 37–45; 8. 3–12; 9. 24–7; 11. 2–40.
5. Dan. 2. 39, 40; 7. 2–14; 10. 1–11. 1.
6. Dan. 4. 10; 7. 9; 8. 1, 2, 15, 17; 9. 1, 2; 10. 4–6.
7. Dan. 9. 2, 3, 21–4 (REB).
8. Dan. 2. 18, 19, 28, 30, 47; cf. 2. 1–11; 4. 4–18; 5. 5–9.
9. Dan. 2. 16, 24, 30, 36, 45; 4. 18, 24; 5. 16, 26.
10. Dan. 2. 2–23, 30; 4. 9, 18; 5. 11, 12, 14.

This kind of exegesis (like other features of the book of Daniel) is already foreshadowed in Zechariah 1–8, where an angel plays the part of the interpreter and discloses the meaning of the prophet's mysterious visions.[11] It is plausible to suspect here an influence from the Babylonians' practice of divination, by which, during their time in exile, the Jews were evidently attracted.[12] To this general background we may add the fascination the later Jewish scribal tradition found in secret and mysterious writings. Wisdom, for example, is praised because 'she knows the past, she can infer what is yet to come; she understands the subtleties of argument and the solving of hard questions; she can read signs and portents and foretell what the different times and seasons will bring about.'[13]

However, the most illuminating parallel is provided by the Dead Sea Scrolls of the Qumran community. One of the first scrolls to be published after their discovery in 1947 gives a detailed commentary on the first two chapters of Habakkuk and here it is explained that the prophet himself did not understand the secret meaning of his oracles; the disclosure of that had to await the God-given interpretation of the Teacher of Righteousness – the community's appointed leader:

> And God told Habakkuk to write down that which would happen to the final generation, but He did not make known to him when time would come to an end. And as for that which He said, *That he who reads may read it speedily*: interpreted this concerns the Teacher of Righteousness, to whom God made known all the mysteries of the words of His servants the Prophets.[14]

With that detachment from reality which nurtures the characteristic mentality of sects, the members of the Qumran community were taught to believe that the imminent end of

---

11. Zech. 1. 9, 19, 20; 2. 3; 4. 4–6, 11–14; 5. 6, 10, 11; 6. 4, 5.
12. See pp. 119–20.
13. Wisd. 8. 8 (REB); cf. Ecclus. 39. 1–3; II Esd. 14. 46–8.
14. Commentary on Habakkuk, VII, 1–5 (translation by G. Vermes).

the world was something they could welcome with eager expectation.

The book of Daniel is comparably sectarian, secretive and confident in its version of the end of history:

> At that time there will appear Michael the great captain,
> who stands guarding your fellow countrymen;
> and there will be a period of anguish such as has never been
>   known
> ever since they became a nation till that moment.
> But at that time your people will be delivered,
> everyone whose name is entered in the book:
> many of those who sleep in the dust of the earth will awake,
> some to everlasting life
> and some to the reproach of eternal abhorrence.
> The wise leaders will shine like the bright vault of heaven,
> and those who have guided the people in the true path
> will be like the stars for ever and ever.
>
> But you, Daniel, keep the words secret and seal the book until
> the time of the end. Many will rush to and fro, trying to gain
> such knowledge.[15]

The kinship between the Qumran community and the group for which the book of Daniel was written is confirmed by the conviction in both that the End was imminent. This is declared to be the meaning of Daniel's dream about the four beasts, symbolizing the nations, in chapter 7:

> As I looked,
>   thrones were placed
>   and one that was ancient of days took his seat;
>   his raiment was white as snow,
>   and the hair of his head like pure wool;
>   his throne was fiery flames,
>   its wheels were burning fire.

15. Dan. 12. 1–4 (REB).

> A stream of fire issued
>   and came forth from before him;
> a thousand thousands served him,
>   and ten thousand times ten
>   thousand stood before him;
> the court sat in judgement,
>   and the books were opened.

> I looked then because of the sound of the great words which the horn was speaking. And as I looked, the beast was slain, and its body destroyed and given over to be burned with fire.
> As for the rest of the beasts, their dominion was taken away, but their lives were prolonged for a season and a time.
>   I saw in the night visions,
>   and behold, with the clouds of heaven
>   there came one like a son of man,
>   and he came to the Ancient of Days
>   and was presented before him.
> And to him was given dominion and glory and kingdom, that all peoples, nations, languages should serve him; his dominion is an everlasting dominion, which shall not pass away, and his kingdom one that shall not be destroyed.[16]

The interpretation of Nebuchadnezzar's dream about the monstrous image in chapter 2 conveys the same message:

> There is a God in heaven who reveals mysteries, and he has made known to King Nebuchadnezzar what will be in the latter days . . . And in the days of those kings the God of heaven will set up a kingdom which shall never be destroyed, nor shall its sovereignty be left to another people. It shall break in pieces all these kingdoms and bring them to an end, and it shall stand for ever . . . A great God has made known to the king what shall be hereafter.[17]

16. Dan. 7. 9–14.
17. Dan. 2. 28, 44, 45.

At a time when loyal Jews were provoked to withdraw into sectarian groups and the practice of their religion was threatened politically, the prophetic scriptures were found to be alive with a message of hope. Whether 'apocalyptic' writing had played any significant part in the religious life of the post-exilic community before the crisis created by Antiochus Epiphanes, or whether it was, in fact, just this crisis which converted it from being a remote esoteric pursuit into a powerful pastoral instrument, it is impossible to discover. In either case, with the book of Daniel there emerges in the received tradition a new and oddly bookish kind of writing intended to comfort the faithful. Whereas the old prophets had presented the action of God in history as making *urgent demands* for obedience, those who interpreted their oracles in the apocalypses present it as offering *imminent succour* by direct divine intervention. This development, it would seem, was the product of four main factors: faith in the sovereignty of God; experience of suffering and rejection; a detailed (if perverse) study of the prophetic scriptures; and the distinctive psychology of a close-knit sectarian group, which enabled its members to believe that the world was about to be wound up for their exclusive benefit. Apocalyptic movements have arisen repeatedly in religious history when these four factors have emerged in combination.

In its final form, the book of Daniel addresses a group of the Elect, which resembled in many ways the contemporaneous community of Qumran, in which the 'wise' attempted, by an esoteric interpretation of scripture, to validate their claim to be the True Israel living on the threshold of the Final Age. It was in such a theological milieu that the first Christians came to articulate their belief.

THE EARLY CHURCH

The New Testament has two apocalypses – the Revelation of John and the so-called little apocalypse of Mark 13. The Revelation of John was a response to the persecution of the Christian community (probably towards the end of the first century)[18] and represented as the disclosure of Jesus to John through an angel: 'The revelation of Jesus Christ, which God gave him to show to his servants what must soon take place; and he made it known by sending his angel to his servant John.'[19] The author's purpose was to assure the faithful that their suffering would soon be ended, because the time of fulfilment was near. This would take the form of the Second Coming of Jesus as judge and redeemer: 'Behold, he is coming with the clouds, and every eye will see him . . . He who gave this testimony says: "Yes, I am coming soon!" Amen. Come Lord Jesus.'[20]

Persecution, similarly, was the occasion of the apocalypse of Mark 13 and, in language often indebted to the book of Daniel,[21] the suffering of Christians is interpreted as the first birth-pangs of the New Age. The actual arrival of the New Age is described almost entirely in phrases culled from the prophetic scriptures:

> But in those days, after that tribulation, the sun will be darkened, and the moon will not give its light, and the stars will be falling from heaven, and the powers in the heavens will be shaken. And then they will see the Son of man coming in clouds with great power and glory. And then he will send out the angels, and gather his elect from the four winds, from the ends of the earth to the ends of heaven.[22]

The early Church, it seems, came to this form of expectation by interpreting the resurrection of Jesus in terms of the apocalyptic tradition it had inherited about the restoration of Israel in the Final Age.

Paul, too, shared the general belief that the Final Age was imminent and would be inaugurated by the Second

18. Rev. 2. 13; 3. 10; 6. 9; 14. 9–12.
19. Rev. 1. 1.
20. Rev. 1.7; 22.20.
21. Mark 13. 14; cf. Dan. 11. 31; 12. 11.
22. Mark 13. 24–6; cf. Joel 2. 10; Isa. 13. 10; 34. 4; Dan. 7. 13.

Coming of Christ. His most explicit statement comes in his attempt to reassure the Thessalonians about what will happen to those Christians who were no longer alive on the Last Day:

> For this we declare to you by the word of the Lord, that we who are alive, who are left until the coming of the Lord, shall not precede those who have fallen asleep. For the Lord himself will descend from heaven with a cry of command, with the archangel's call, and with the sound of the trumpet of God. And the dead in Christ will rise first; then we who are alive, who are left, shall be caught up together with them in the clouds to meet the Lord in the air; and so we shall always be with the Lord. Therefore comfort one another with these words.[23]

Further evidence that the framework of Paul's thinking was inherited from Jewish expectation is to be found in the importance he attached to the inclusion of the Gentiles in the restored community of the Final Age.[24] This was a theme well represented in the prophetic scriptures.[25]

Just how soon the early Church expected the coming of the Final Age is unambiguously confirmed by the embarrassed admission of the author of II Peter (writing about the end of the century) that it had fallen behind schedule. His solution to the problem is to bluster, blackguard the sceptics and fiddle the time-scale:

> Scoffers will come in the last days with scoffing, following their own passions and saying, 'Where is the promise of his coming? For ever since the fathers fell asleep, all things have continued as they were from the beginning of creation . . .' But do not ignore this one fact, beloved, that with the Lord one day is as a thousand years, and a thousand years as one day. The Lord is not slow about his promise as some count

23. I Thess. 4. 15–18; cf. I Cor. 15. 51, 52; 7. 29; Rom. 13. 11, 12; Matt. 16. 27, 28.
24. Rom. 11. 13–16, 25; 15. 14–21.
25. Isa. 49. 5, 6; 56. 1–8; 66. 18–24; Mic. 4.1–4; cf. Tobit 14. 6, 7; see pp. 143–5.

slowness, but is forbearing toward you, not wishing that any should perish, but that all should reach repentance.[26]

Belief in the Second Coming has given concern to expositors and apologists ever since this first attempt at explanation.

JESUS AND PROPHECY

It is clear that the leaders of the early Church were convinced that Jesus was the key to the scriptures and, in particular, the predictions they discovered in the books of the prophets. The attitude of Jesus himself to Jewish expectation is more difficult to determine. The ambiguity is illustrated by his relationship to John the Baptist, the charismatic prophet, who introduced him to the current excitement about God's imminent coming in judgement, and by whom he was baptized:

> In those days came John the Baptist, preaching in the wilderness of Judaea, 'Repent, for the kingdom of heaven is at hand.' This is he who was spoken of by the prophet Isaiah when he said, 'The voice of one crying in the wilderness: Prepare the way of the Lord, Make his paths straight.'[27]

John called for repentance before 'the wrath to come' and declared that 'even now the axe is laid to the root of the trees'.[28]

Up to a point, it appears that Jesus accepted John's teaching, as we learn not only from his direct endorsement of his ministry,[29] but indirectly from the anxious determination, reflected in the gospel tradition, to make it clear that John was not dominant.[30] There can be no doubt, however, that Jesus

---

26. II Pet. 3. 3–9.
27. Matt. 3. 1–3.
28. Matt. 3. 7–10.
29. Matt. 11. 7–15.
30. Matt. 3. 14; 11. 11; John 1. 19–37; 3. 25–30; cf. Acts 18. 24–6.

differed fundamentally from John and from the outlook he represented. He was no ascetic;[31] he ate and drank with tax-gatherers and sinners;[32] instead of preaching the urgent need for repentance before the coming judgement, he simply invited the lost and the wicked to share through him the new life of the Kingdom of God.[33]

> And he came to Nazareth, where he had been brought up; and he went to the synagogue, as his custom was, on the sabbath day. And he stood up to read; and there was given to him the book of the prophet Isaiah. He opened the book and found the place where it was written,
>
> > 'The Spirit of the Lord is upon me,
> > because he has anointed me to preach
> >   good news to the poor.
> > He has sent me to proclaim release to
> >   the captives
> > and recovering of sight to the blind,
> > to set at liberty those who are oppressed,
> > to proclaim the acceptable year of the Lord.'
>
> And he closed the book, and gave it back to the attendant, and sat down; and the eyes of all in the synagogue were fixed on him. And he began to say to them, *'Today this scripture has been fulfilled in your hearing.'*[34]

There is a good deal of evidence to show that Jesus was looked upon by his contemporaries as 'a prophet mighty in deed and word before God and all the people'.[35] His healing of the widow's son at Nain caused a great stir among the crowd, 'and they glorified God, saying, "A great prophet has arisen among us!" and "God has visited his people!" And this report

31. Matt. 11. 18, 19; Mark 2. 18–20.
32. Mark 2. 13–17; Matt. 21. 31, 32.
33. Matt. 22. 1–10.
34. Luke 4. 16–21; cf. Isa. 61. 1, 2.
35. Luke 24. 19.

concerning him spread through the whole of Judaea and all the surrounding country.'[36] Similarly, the man born blind, when he was healed by Jesus, could only conclude that 'He is a prophet.'[37] It is not surprising, therefore, that the crowds who watched the Triumphal Entry into Jerusalem at the beginning of the last week of Jesus' life, answered the general inquiry, 'Who is this?' by affirming, 'This is the prophet Jesus from Nazareth of Galilee.'[38] And the Pharisees hesitated to arrest him the following day, because the crowds 'held him to be a prophet'.[39]

More important, however, than Jesus being called a 'prophet' (which, we should bear in mind, depends on the popular understanding of prophecy in the first century AD), is the unmistakable evidence that his own vocation is illuminated by that of the great prophets of the Old Testament. Like them, he was conscious that he had been sent by God:

> Whoever receives one such child in my name receives me; and whoever receives me receives not me, but him that sent me.[40]

Conversely, the people's rejection of him meant no less than their rejection of God, as he is represented as affirming in the Fourth Gospel:

> He who rejects me and does not receive my sayings has a judge; the word that I have spoken will be his judge on the last day. For I have not spoken on my own authority; the Father who sent me has himself given me commandment what to say and what to speak.[41]

This is the authentic idiom of prophecy and in line with

36. Luke 7. 16, 17; cf. 7. 39.
37. John 9. 17; cf. 4. 19.
38. Matt. 21. 11.
39. Matt. 21. 46.
40. Mark 9. 37; cf. Matt. 10. 40; 15. 24; John 13. 20; 6. 44; 7. 16; Isa. 6. 8; Jer. 26. 15; 28. 15.
41. John 12. 48, 49; cf. 5. 23; 15. 23; Luke 10. 16; cf. Exod. 16. 8.

Micaiah's declaration: 'As the LORD lives, what the LORD says to me, that I will speak.'[42] Like the great prophets, Jesus was a man set under authority[43] and entrusted with authority,[44] known of God[45] and consecrated by him,[46] charged with an inescapable and heart-breaking mission. It is as difficult to find direct evidence of the personal consciousness of Jesus, as it is to penetrate the inner nature of the prophets' awareness. We know, however, that both Jesus and the prophets found temptation in the path of their vocation and knew the price of obedience. We need only recall the anguish of Jeremiah:

> For whenever I speak, I cry out,
> I shout, 'Violence and destruction!'
> For the word of the LORD has become for me
> a reproach and derision all day long.
> If I say, 'I will not mention him,
> or speak any more in his name,'
> there is in my heart as it were a burning fire
> shut up in my bones,
> and I am weary with holding it in,
> and I cannot.[47]

With this in mind, we can better appreciate the agony of Jesus:

> I came to cast fire upon the earth; and would that it were already kindled! I have a baptism to be baptized with; and how I am constrained until it is accomplished! Do you think that I have come to give peace on earth? No, I tell you, but rather division.[48]

There is, however, a significant difference between Jeremiah

42. I Kgs. 22. 14; cf. Jer. 1. 7, 17 and see pp. 54–6.
43. John 4. 34; 5. 30; Amos 3. 8.
44. Matt. 28. 18; John 3. 35; 5. 27; Jer. 1. 10.
45. John 10. 15; Jer. 12. 3.
46. John 10. 36; Jer. 1. 5.
47. Jer. 20. 8, 9.
48. Luke 12. 49–51.

and Jesus. Jeremiah still clings to a residuum of self-will, which Jesus has extirpated in perfect devotion to the Father:

> O LORD, thou knowest;
> remember me and visit me,
> and take vengeance for me on
>   my persecutors.
> In thy forbearance take me not away;
>   know that for thy sake I bear reproach.
> Thy words were found, and I ate them,
>   and thy words became to me a joy
>   and the delight of my heart;
> for I am called by thy name,
>   O LORD, God of hosts.[49]

The agony in Gethsemane leads to a very different conclusion:

> And he said to them, 'My soul is very sorrowful, even to death; remain here, and watch.' And going a little farther, he fell on the ground and prayed that, if it were possible, the hour might pass from him. And he said, 'Abba, Father, all things are possible to thee; remove this cup from me; yet not what I will, but what thou wilt.'[50]

Whereas the prophets rebelled from time to time against the personal and moral obligations of their vocation, Jesus never rebelled. Like the prophets, he heard and proclaimed the Word of the Lord, but, unlike the prophets, he was in life always as good as his word. In his obedience to God, Jesus had given himself as 'a covenant to the people'[51] and actualized Jeremiah's faith in the inauguration of a New Covenant – that New Covenant by which the New Israel of God was to be established.[52]

49. Jer. 15. 15, 16.
50. Mark 14. 34–6.
51. Isa. 42. 6; 49. 8; Zech. 9. 11; I Cor. 11. 25; Luke 22. 20; Mark 14. 24; Matt. 26. 28.
52. Jer. 31. 31–4; cf. Heb. 8. 8–13; II Cor. 3. 6; 5. 17; Col. 2. 9, 10; see pp. 113–14.

In Jesus, the great prophets' awareness of God found fulfilment. The righteousness in terms of which they had spoken of the Kingdom of God became in the life and teaching of Jesus a present demand. His conviction that the Kingdom was already confronting people with a call to absolute righteousness is the assumption on which, for example, the whole Sermon on the Mount is founded:

> You have heard that it was said, 'You shall love your neighbour and hate your enemy.' But *I say to you*, Love your enemies and pray for those who persecute you, so that you may be sons of your Father who is in heaven.[53]

This firm but quiet assumption of authority, for which (especially in the Fourth Gospel) the term 'kingship' is occasionally used, is the evidence of Jesus' personal participation in the central theme of his teaching – the inauguration of the kingly Rule of God.[54] What was of faith and the future for the prophets was for Jesus a present and overwhelming reality:

> Blessed are the eyes which see what you see! For I tell you that many prophets and kings desired to see what you see, and did not see it, and to hear what you hear, and did not hear it.[55]

> Jesus came into Galilee, preaching the gospel of God, and saying, 'The time is fulfilled, and the kingdom of God is at hand.'[56]

The whole of the New Testament is a commentary on the proclamation that 'the time is fulfilled'. The Christian com-

53. Matt. 5. 43–5; cf. 5. 22, 28, 34, 39; Mark 1. 27.
54. Luke 19. 38; Matt. 21. 5; John 12. 12–16; cf. Zech. 9. 9; John 1. 49; 18. 37; 19. 15, 21, 22; Rev. 17. 14; 19. 16.
55. Luke 10. 23, 24.
56. Mark 1. 14, 15; cf. Matt. 4. 17; 10. 7; Luke 10. 9; 17. 21.

munity was founded on the conviction that in the life, death, and resurrection of Jesus, God had decisively accomplished that purpose which he disclosed in history when he called Israel to be his people.[57] There were, indeed, those who continued to think of the Last Day as a future event,[58] but even they held that the time was 'very short', thus affirming their recognition that in Jesus the decisive event had already taken place: 'The hour is coming and now is.'[59]

The New Testament is unintelligible until we have kept company with the prophets of the Old Testament, grasped their conception of God's purpose in Israel's calling and history, understood their conviction concerning Israel's judgement and salvation, and shared their vision of the new People of God to be established on that day when God reigned as King of the whole world. The New Testament proclaims that God-in-Christ has accomplished the purpose disclosed in Israel's history, attained the end to which it was directed, and initiated the fulfilment to which the prophets looked forward in faith.

57. See the records of the earliest apostolic preaching in Acts 13. 17–41; 2. 14–39; 3. 12–26; 10. 36–43; cf. I Cor. 15. 1–7.

58. Acts 1. 11; 3. 19–21; 10. 42; I Thess. 4. 15–17; I Cor. 15. 51, 52; 16. 22; Rom. 2. 16; I Pet. 1. 5; 4. 7.

59. I John 2. 18; Matt. 16. 28; I Cor. 7. 29; Rev. 22. 6, 7, 20; John 5. 25.

BIBLIOGRAPHY

The books marked ** are especially recommended as an introduction to their subject and those marked * are also suitable for the earlier stages of study.

GENERAL

** May, H. G., G. N. S. Hunt and R. W. Hamilton (eds.) *Oxford Bible Atlas*. Oxford, Oxford University Press, 1974

** Rogerson, John and Philip Davies. *The Old Testament World*. Cambridge, Cambridge University Press, 1989

** Hayes, J. H. and C. R. Holladay. *Biblical Exegesis: A Beginner's Handbook*. London, SCM Press, 1983

* Anderson, B. W. *The Living World of the Old Testament*. Harlow, Longmans, 1967

Bright, J. *A History of Israel*. London, SCM Press, 1981

Hayes, J. H. and J. M. Miller (eds.) *Israelite and Judaean History*. London, SCM Press, 1977

1. MAKING SENSE OF THE OLD TESTAMENT

** Bowden, J. *What About the Old Testament?* London, SCM Press, 1969

** Rogerson, J. (ed.) *Beginning Old Testament Study*. London, SPCK, 1983

* Barton, J. *Reading the Old Testament. Method in Biblical Study*. London, SPCK, 1984

* Coggins, R. *Introducing the Old Testament*. Oxford, Oxford University Press, 1990

* Anderson, G. W. 'The History of Biblical Interpretation' in *The Interpreter's One-Volume Commentary on the Bible*, ed. C. M. Laymon. London, Collins, 1972

* Evans, C. F. *Is 'Holy Scripture' Christian?* London, SCM Press, 1971

Kraeling, E. G. *The Old Testament since the Reformation.* Cambridge, Lutterworth Press, 1955

* Barr, J. *The Bible in the Modern World.* London, SCM Press, 1973

2. THE BOOKS OF THE PROPHETS

** Emmerson, Grace (ed.) *Prophets and Poets.* Oxford, The Bible Reading Fellowship, 1994

* Eissfeldt, O. 'The Prophetic Literature' in *The Old Testament and Modern Study*, ed. H. H. Rowley. Oxford, Clarendon Press, 1951

Blenkinsopp, J. *A History of Prophecy in Israel.* London, SPCK, 1984

Sawyer, J. F. A. *Prophecy and the Prophets of the Old Testament.* Oxford, Oxford University Press, 1987

Coggins, R., A. Phillips and M. Knibb (eds.) *Israel's Prophetic Tradition.* Cambridge, Cambridge University Press, 1982

Eissfeldt, O. *The Old Testament: An Introduction*, trans. P. R. Ackroyd. Oxford, Blackwell Publishers, 1965

Fohrer, G. *Introduction to the Old Testament*, trans. D. Green. London, SPCK, 1970

Kaiser, O. *Introduction to the Old Testament*, trans. J. Sturdy. Oxford, Blackwell Publishers, 1975

Soggin, J. A. *Introduction to the Old Testament*, trans. J. Bowden. London, SCM Press, 1989

* Heaton, E. W. *The Hebrew Kingdoms* (New Clarendon Bible). Oxford, Oxford University Press, 1968

* Ackroyd, P. R. *Israel under Babylon and Persia* (New Clarendon Bible). Oxford, Oxford University Press, 1970

* Russell, D. S. *The Jews from Alexander to Herod* (New Clarendon Bible). Oxford, Oxford University Press, 1967

3. THE VOCATION OF THE PROPHETS

** Mowvley, H. *Guide to Old Testament Prophecy.* Cambridge, Lutterworth Press, 1979

174   *Old Testament Prophets*

* Rowley, H. H. 'The Nature of Old Testament Prophecy in the Light of Present Study' in *The Servant of the Lord*. Oxford, Blackwell Publishers, 1965
* Smith, W. R. *The Prophets of Israel*. London, A. & C. Black, 1895
** Scott, R. B. Y. *The Relevance of the Prophets*. New York, Macmillan, 1968
* Clements, R. E. *Prophecy and Covenant*. London, SCM Press, 1965
** Muilenburg, J. 'Old Testament Prophecy' in *Peake's Commentary*, ed. M. Black and H. H. Rowley. Walton-on-Thames, Thomas Nelson & Sons, 1962
Johnson, A. R. *The Cultic Prophet in Ancient Israel*. Cardiff, University of Wales Press, 1962
Lindblom, J. *Prophecy in Ancient Israel*. Oxford, Blackwell Publishers, 1962
Ross, J. F. 'The Prophet as Yahweh's Messenger' in *Israel's Prophetic Heritage*, ed. B. W. Anderson and W. Harrelson. London, SCM Press, 1962
Stacey, W. D. *Prophetic Drama in the Old Testament*. Manchester, Epworth Press, 1990
Davidson, R. *The Courage to Doubt: Exploring an Old Testament Theme*. London, SCM Press, 1983
von Rad, G. *Old Testament Theology*, vol. 2, trans. D. M. G. Stalker. Harlow, Essex, Oliver & Boyd, 1965
Vriezen, T. C. *The Religion of Ancient Israel*, trans. H. Hoskins. Cambridge, Lutterworth Press, 1967

4. THE PREACHING OF THE PROPHETS

* Sandmel S. *The Enjoyment of Scripture*. Oxford, Oxford University Press, 1973
Caird, G. B. *The Language and Imagery of the Bible*. London, Gerald Duckworth & Co., 1980
Anderson, G. W. (ed.) *Tradition and Interpretation*. Oxford, Clarendon Press, 1979
Westermann, C. *Basic Forms of Prophetic Speech*, trans. H. C. White. Cambridge, Lutterworth Press, 1967

* Clements, R. E., *Prophecy and Tradition*. Oxford, Blackwell Publishers, 1975

* von Rad, G. *The Message of the Prophets*, trans. D. M. G. Stalker. London, SCM Press, 1968

Rowley, H. H. 'The Prophets and the Cult' in *Worship in Ancient Israel*. London, SPCK, 1967

* Fohrer, G. *History of Israelite Religion*, trans. D. E. Green. London, SPCK, 1973

Davies, E. W. *Prophecy and Ethics: Isaiah and the Ethical Traditions of Israel*. Sheffield, JSOT Press, 1981

* Porteous, N. W. 'The Basis of the Ethical Teaching of the Prophets' and 'Ritual and Righteousness' in *Living the Mystery*. Oxford, Blackwell Publishers, 1967

Whybray, R. N. *The Intellectual Tradition in the Old Testament*. Berlin, W. de Gruyter, 1974

Heaton, E. W. *The School Tradition of the Old Testament*. Oxford, Clarendon Press, 1994

5. JUDGEMENT WITHOUT PROMISE

Amos

** Auld, A. G. *Amos* (Old Testament Guides). Sheffield, JSOT Press, 1986

** McKeating, H. *Amos, Hosea, Micah* (Cambridge Commentary on the New English Bible). Cambridge, Cambridge University Press, 1971

Mays, J. L. *Amos* (Old Testament Library Commentary). London, SCM Press, 1969

van der Woude, A. S. 'Three Classical Prophets' in *Israel's Prophetic Tradition*, ed. R. Coggins, A. Phillips and M. Knibb. Cambridge, Cambridge University Press, 1982

Barton, J. *Amos's Oracles Against the Nations*. Cambridge, Cambridge University Press, 1980

Terrien, S. L. 'Amos and Wisdom' in *Israel's Prophetic Heritage*, ed. B. W. Anderson and W. Harrelson. London, SCM Press, 1962

Coote, R. B. *Amos Among the Prophets: Composition and Theology*. Philadelphia, Fortress Press, 1981

Isaiah

Scott, R. B. Y. Commentary in *The Interpreter's Bible*, vol. 5. New York, Abingdon Press, 1956

Clements, R. E. *Isaiah 1–39* (New Century Bible Commentary), London, Marshall, Morgan, Scott, 1980

** Herbert, A. S. *Isaiah 1–39* (Cambridge Commentary on the New English Bible). Cambridge, Cambridge University Press, 1973

Kaiser, O. *Isaiah 1–12* and *Isaiah 13–29* (Old Testament Library Commentary), trans. R. A. Wilson. London, SCM Press, 1983 and 1980

Stacey, D. *Isaiah 1–39* (Epworth Commentaries). Manchester, Epworth Press, 1993

McKane, W. *Prophets and Wise Men*. London, SCM Press, 1965

Whedbee, J. W. *Isaiah and Wisdom*. New York, Abingdon Press, 1971

* Vriezen, T. C. 'Essentials of the Theology of Isaiah' in *Israel's Prophetic Heritage*, ed. B. W. Anderson and W. Harrelson. London, SCM Press, 1962

Micah

** Mason, R. A. *Micah, Nahum, Obadiah* (Old Testament Guides). Sheffield, JSOT Press, 1991

Mays, J. L. *Micah* (Old Testament Library Commentary). London, SCM Press, 1971

Wolfe, R. E. Commentary in *The Interpreter's Bible*, vol. 6. New York, Abingdon Press, 1956

van der Woude, A. S. 'Three Classical Prophets' in *Israel's Prophetic Tradition*, ed. R. Coggins, A. Phillips and M. Knibb. Cambridge, Cambridge University Press, 1982

6. SALVATION THROUGH JUDGEMENT

Hosea

** Davies, G. I. *Hosea* (Old Testament Guides). Sheffield, Sheffield Academic Press, 1993

** Ackroyd, P. R. Commentary in *Peake's Commentary*, ed.

M. Black and H. H. Rowley. Walton-on-Thames, Thomas Nelson & Sons, 1962

Davies, G. I. *Hosea* (New Century Bible Commentary). London, Marshall Pickering 1992

Mays, J. L. *Hosea* (Old Testament Library Commentary). London, SCM Press, 1969

** Robinson, H. W. *Two Hebrew Prophets*. Cambridge, Lutterworth Press, 1948

 * Anderson, B. W. *The Eighth-Century Prophets*. London, SPCK, 1979

Jeremiah

** Carroll, R. P. *Jeremiah* (Old Testament Guides). Sheffield, JSOT Press, 1989

** Nicholson, E. W. *Jeremiah 1–25* and *Jeremiah 26–52* (Cambridge Commentary on the New English Bible). Cambridge, Cambridge University Press, 1973 and 1975

Jones, D. R. *Jeremiah* (New Century Bible Commentary). London, Marshall Pickering, 1992

Nicholson, E. W. *Preaching to the Exiles*. Oxford, Blackwell Publishers, 1970

Carroll, R. P. *Jeremiah* (Old Testament Library Commentary). London, SCM Press, 1986

 * Bright, J. *Jeremiah* (The Anchor Bible). London, Doubleday, 1965

Skinner, J. *Prophecy and Religion*. Cambridge, Cambridge University Press, 1922

** Robinson, H. W. *The Cross in the Old Testament*. London, SCM Press, 1955

Overholt, T. W. *The Threat of Falsehood*. London, SCM Press, 1970

7. SALVATION AFTER JUDGEMENT

Second Isaiah

** Whybray, R. N. *The Second Isaiah* (Old Testament Guides). Sheffield, JSOT Press, 1983

** Ackroyd, P. R. Commentary in *The Interpreter's One-*

Volume Commentary on The Bible, ed. C. M. Laymon. London, Collins, 1972

Whybray, R. N. *Isaiah 40–66* (New Century Bible Commentary). London, Oliphants, 1975

Muilenburg, J. Commentary in *The Interpreter's Bible*, vol. 5. New York, Abingdon Press, 1956

Westermann, C. *Isaiah 40–66* (Old Testament Library Commentary), trans. D. M. G. Stalker. London, SCM Press, 1969

North, C. R. *The Second Isaiah*. Oxford, The Clarendon Press, 1964

Ackroyd, P. R. *Exile and Restoration*. London, SCM Press, 1968

* Rowley, H. H. *The Servant of the Lord*. Cambridge, Lutterworth Press, 1965

Ezekiel

** McKeating, H. *Ezekiel* (Old Testament Guides). Sheffield, Sheffield Academic Press, 1993

May, H. G. Commentary in *The Interpreter's Bible*, vol. 6. New York, Abingdon Press, 1956

** Muilenburg, J. Commentary in *Peake's Commentary*, ed. M. Black and H. H. Rowley. Walton-on-Thames, Thomas Nelson & Sons, 1962

** Carley, K. W. *The Book of the Prophet Ezekiel* (Cambridge Commentary on the New English Bible). Cambridge, Cambridge University Press, 1974

Carley, K. W. *Ezekiel Among the Prophets*. London, SCM Press, 1975

Wevers, J. W. *Ezekiel* (New Century Bible Commentary). London, Oliphants, 1969

Eichrodt, W. *Ezekiel* (Old Testament Library Commentary). London, SCM Press, 1970

** Robinson, H. W. *Two Hebrew Prophets*. Cambridge, Lutterworth Press, 1948

Rowley, H. H. 'The Book of Ezekiel in Modern Study' in *Men of God*. Walton-on-Thames, Thomas Nelson & Sons, 1963

8. SALVATION IN THE RESTORED COMMUNITY

Ackroyd, P. R. *Exile and Restoration*. London, SCM Press, 1968

* Ackroyd, P. R. *Israel Under Babylon and Persia* (New Clarendon Bible). Oxford, Oxford University Press, 1970

* Ball, E. 'Zephaniah' in *A Dictionary of Biblical Interpretation*, ed. R. J. Coggins and J. L. Houlden. London, SCM Press, 1990

** Mason, R. A. *Zephaniah, Habakkuk, Joel* (Old Testament Guides). Sheffield, JSOT Press, 1994

** Williamson, H. G. M. *Ezra and Nehemiah* (Old Testament Guides). Sheffield, JSOT Press, 1987

Haggai and Zechariah 1–8

** Coggins, R. J. *Haggai, Zechariah, Malachi* (Old Testament Guides). Sheffield, JSOT Press, 1987

Mason, R. A. *The Books of Haggai, Zechariah and Malachi* (Cambridge Commentary on the New English Bible). Cambridge, Cambridge University Press, 1977

Petersen, D. L. *Haggai and Zechariah 1–8* (Old Testament Library Commentary). London, SCM Press, 1985

Isaiah 56–66

** Emmerson G. I. *Isaiah 56–66* (Old Testament Guides). Sheffield, JSOT Press, 1994

** Herbert, A. S. *Isaiah 40–66* (Cambridge Commentary on the New English Bible). Cambridge, Cambridge University Press, 1975

Westermann, C. *Isaiah 40–66* (Old Testament Library Commentary), trans. D. M. G. Stalker. London, SCM Press, 1969

Muilenburg, J. Commentary in *The Interpreter's Bible*, vol. 5, New York, Abingdon Press, 1956

9. THE SCRIPTURE OF THE PROPHETS

Barton, J. *Oracles of God: Perceptions of Ancient Prophecy in*

Israel After the Exile. London, Darton, Longman and Todd, 1986

Mason, R. A. *Preaching the Tradition: Homily and Hermeneutics After the Exile.* Cambridge, Cambridge University Press, 1990

Collins, T. *The Mantle of Elijah: The Redaction Criticism of the Prophetical Books.* Sheffield, Sheffield Academic Press, 1993

** Jones, G. *1 and 2 Chronicles* (Old Testament Guides). Sheffield, JSOT Press, 1993

Blenkinsopp, J. *A History of Prophecy in Israel.* London, SPCK, 1984

10. PROPHETIC FOREKNOWLEDGE OF THE IMMINENT END

** Davies, P. R. *Daniel* (Old Testament Guides). Sheffield, JSOT Press, 1985

** Barr, J. Commentary on 'Daniel' in *Peake's Commentary*, ed. M. Black and H. H. Rowley. Walton-on-Thames, Thomas Nelson & Sons, 1962

** Heaton, E. W. *The Book of Daniel* (Torch Commentary). London, SCM Press, 1956

Porteous, N. W. *The Book of Daniel* (Old Testament Library Commentary). London, SCM Press, 1979

Bruce, F. F. 'The Book of Daniel and the Qumran Community' in *Neotestamentica et Semitica*, ed. E. E. Ellis and M. Wilcox. Edinburgh, T & T Clark, 1969

 Biblical Exegesis in the Qumran Texts. London, Tyndale Press, 1960

Vermes, G. *The Dead Sea Scrolls in English.* Harmondsworth, Middlesex, Penguin Books, 1987

 Jesus the Jew. London, Collins, 1973

 Jesus and the World of Judaism. London, SCM Press, 1983

 The Religion of Jesus the Jew. London, SCM Press, 1993

Russell, D. S. *Divine Disclosure: An Introduction to Jewish Apocalyptic.* London, SCM Press, 1992

Rowland, C. *The Open Heaven. A Study of Apocalyptic in Judaism and Early Christianity*. London, SPCK, 1982

Dodd, C. H. *The Parables of the Kingdom*. Hitchin, Herts., James Nisbet & Co., 1961

According to the Scriptures. Hitchin, Herts., James Nisbet & Co., 1952

The Founder of Christianity. London, Collier-Macmillan, 1970

'Jesus as Teacher and Prophet' in *Mysterium Christi*, eds. G. K. A. Bell and A. Deismann. Harlow, Essex, Longmans, 1930

Sanders, E. P. *Jesus and Judaism*. London, SCM Press, 1985

The Historical Figure of Jesus, Harmondsworth, Penguin Books, 1993

Indexes

Index of Biblical References

Index of Subjects